COUNTRY LIVING
INNOVATION
AND DESIGN

Contents

COUNTRY LIVING
INNOVATION
AND DESIGN

what is it? | what is it worth?

Joe L. Rosson

Helaine Fendelman

House of Collectibles

New York   Toronto   London   Sydney   Auckland

House of Collectibles and colophon are registered trademarks of Random House, Inc.

RANDOM HOUSE is a registered trademark of Random House, Inc.

Country Living is a trademark of Hearst Communications, Inc.

This book is available at special discounts for bulk purchases for sales promotions or premiums. Special editions, including personalized covers, excerpts of existing books, and corporate imprints, can be created in large quantities for special needs. For more information, write to Random House, Inc., Special Markets/Premium Sales, 1745 Broadway, MD 6-2, New York, NY 10019 or e-mail specialmarkets@randomhouse.com.

Please address inquiries about electronic licensing of any products for use on a network, in software, or on CD-ROM to the Subsidiary Rights Department, Random House Information Group, fax 212-572-6003.

Visit the House of Collectibles Web site: *www.houseofcollectibles.com*

Visit *Country Living* magazine: *www.countryliving.com*

Library of Congress Cataloging-in-Publication Data

Rosson, Joe.
  Country living : innovation and design : what is it? what is it worth? / Joe L. Rosson, Helaine Fendelman.
    p. cm.
  Includes bibliographical references and index.
  ISBN-13: 978-0-375-72119-9 (trade pbk. : alk. paper)   1. Household appliances—Collectors and collecting—Catalogs.   2. Machinery—Collectors and collecting—Catalogs.   3. Household appliances—Prices—Catalogs.
4. Machinery—Prices—Catalogs. I. Fendelman, Helaine W. II. Title.
  T19.R67 2007
  643'.6075—dc22

                                        2007003270

Printed in China

10 9 8 7 6 5 4 3 2 1

ISBN: 978-0-375-72119-9

RADIOS   107

Acknowledgments

This book would have been nearly impossible to write without the help of some friends—both old and new. Their help was unselfishly given, and we want to thank them for all of their kind assistance.

We suppose we should start by thanking one of our dearest friends—Elaine Tomber-Tindell. This is the lady we sometimes refer to as "Madame Producer" because she produced our television show, *Treasures in Your Attic™*, for years. She thinks we call her "Madame Producer" when we are mad at her, but it is a term of affection and endearment. She is an avid collector, and she is very generous with her treasures.

Next, we want to express our deepest appreciation to Cologne, Germany's Breker Auction Team Koln (Auktionen Uwe Breker) for its support. This auction company calls itself "The Specialist" and indeed it is a world-renowned specialist in technological antiques. It is perhaps the best place in the world to buy and sell technological antiques, and we are grateful for their help.

We also want to thank three other auction houses: Skinner Inc. in Boston and Bolton, Massachusetts; Ivey-Selkirk Auctioneers in St. Louis, Missouri; and Copake Auction Inc. in Copake, New York. All three kindly gave us their support and supplied images that added depth to this book. In addition, we want to express our gratitude to two antiques businesses in New York City that helped us complete this project—Jim Elkind of Lost City Arts and Sandi Berman of Deco Deluxe.

Julian Burke is a collector who opened his house and amazed us with the depth and breadth of his incredible accumulation of radio and television memorabilia. He is a true collector, and very helpful. In addition, we want to thank Roger Welsh and Jennifer Mass for the additions they made to this book, and Rick Crane, whose steadfast support and technical skills have made our job much easier. Finally, we want to dedicate this book to the memory of Jayme McMurry.

Introduction

For many of us who started collecting in the mid- to late twentieth century, our pursuit of things that are "old" is part passion, part pastime—but it is all about objects made at the turn of the twentieth century and before. We are endlessly fascinated with objects from the past, especially those that exhibit fine hand workmanship or artistic expression and speak of quieter, simpler times that have now disappeared.

With the exception of clocks, watches, and the like, we "old school" collectors traditionally have had very little interest in items that are mechanical. We also tend to scorn things that are electric—unless they happen to come with a Tiffany lamp shade on top. But to quote an old song, "the times, they are a-changing," and "new school" collectors have a serious and growing interest in gadgets and devices that are associated both with the past and the "modern" age.

Answering the public's questions the way we do, we have noticed a major upswing in interest in such things as electric fans, sewing machines, typewriters, toasters, and other kitchen gadgets as well as mid-twentieth-century accessories. We are getting questions about "antique" microwave ovens (there is no such thing), and even crock pots and pressure cookers.

In this book, we will not be discussing crock pots, pressure cookers, and microwave ovens because they are not yet of value (with the exception of the very first microwave ovens, which were very expensive when they were new). In addition, we will not be looking into really big objects such as refrigerators and washing machines because these items are so large that few people have the space in their homes to form a collection. This is not to say that there is no interest in these larger items—vintage gas and electric ranges in particular are highly sought after in some parts of the country to be used in the restoration of period kitchens in old houses—but they will not appear on these pages.

What we will be exploring is a wide variety of things mechanical, electrical, and functional that seem to have caught the attention of twenty-first-century collectors, and this includes two of the most important inventions of the twentieth century—radio and television. Much of what will be discussed in these pages would not be possible without electricity and the ability to deliver that commodity to the homes of America and elsewhere. Electricity has a history that is much longer than many might suppose, and it is speculated that even the ancients knew something about the uses of this natural force.

The Greeks knew that if pieces of amber were rubbed with fur, a spark could be produced. When it came time for Europeans to coin a term for this type of energy, they chose the word "electricus," which was derived from the Greek word for amber—"Elektron." Even more intriguing is the so-called "Baghdad Battery," which dates to 250 B.C. and is thought to be a galvanic cell used for producing an electric current that could be used for electroplating precious metals such as silver and gold onto a base metal.

Experimentation with electricity in Europe and America began at least in the sixteenth century and included the work of such men as Alessandro Volta, Michael Faraday, Andre-Marie Ampere, and of course, Benjamin Franklin. Probably the first practical use of electricity was the telegraph, which was based on the electromagnet demonstrated by British inventor William Sturgeon in 1825.

Sturgeon hooked a 7-ounce piece of iron to a single cell battery, which then lifted a 9-pound weight. In 1830, American inventor Joseph Henry built on Sturgeon's demonstration by putting up a mile of wire and then sending an electric current down its length to activate an electromagnet that in turn caused a bell to ring. This is considered the birth of the telegraph.

If you ask most Americans who invented the telegraph, they are likely to respond, Samuel F.B. Morse (1791–1872), but this is open to a great deal of debate. Some say that although Henry pioneered the prototype, it was Morse in 1837 who patented the necessary equipment to make a telegraph system work and later made the telegraph commercially viable. It should also be noted that Baron Schilling created a working electromagnetic telegraph system in 1832, and Sir Charles Wheatstone and Sir William Fothergill patented the telegraph in England in 1837.

Morse and his assistant, Alfred Vail, developed the famous "Morse Code," and in 1835, Morse demonstrated a type of telegraph that recorded telegraphic messages on a moving strip of paper. The first telegraphic message was sent between Washington, D.C., and Baltimore, Maryland, on May 24, 1844, by Morse, who said "What hath God wrought?" The point of all this is that by the time Thomas Alva Edison (1847–1931) was working as an inventor, the concept of electricity moving along a wire doing work was definitely not a new one.

Edison's mother taught him at home until he was 12 and then he went to work on a train selling candy and newspapers to passengers. At 16, the budding genius with no formal education went to work as a telegraph operator.

In 1868, his first creation was a special telegraph designed to record votes, but the intended user, the Massachusetts State Legislature, rejected it and Edison vowed never to invent anything else unless he had a ready market. His first successful invention was an improvement to the stock ticker, which was basically a telegraph that recorded stock exchange prices. This was followed by a quadruplex telegraph system that could simultaneously carry two messages going in each direction on one wire.

Edison decided to become a full-time inventor in 1876 and set up his laboratories in Menlo Park, New Jersey. He began by inventing the phonograph but soon turned his attention to perfecting the incandescent light bulb. The principle for such a device was well known—but establishing a good vacuum in a glass vessel, finding a long-lasting filament, and establishing a reliable electric delivery system were problems that would take a great deal of thought as well as trial and error experimentation to solve.

It is said that Edison tried more than 3,000 different substances before he found one that would work. The principle of the light bulb was established in 1801, when Sir Humphry Davy passed an electric current through platinum strips and made them glow. But these strips did not last long. Over the years, several Europeans produced versions of an incandescent light bulb, but the first practical device was probably the work of German inventor Henrich Gobel. In 1854, he used a carbonized bamboo filament in a vacuum bottle to produce an incandescent light bulb.

Joseph Wilson Swann patented an incandescent light bulb in England in 1878, and he actually began illuminating homes, businesses, and landmarks with his device. In Canada the team of Woodward and Evans came up with an incandescent light bulb that used carbon filaments, and they received Canadian and U.S. patents for their work—but they could not produce their invention commercially.

Edison thought the work of these two Canadians had potential, so he bought their patents before he started work on making his own version of the incandescent light bulb. Edison finally decided to use a carbon filament that went through its first successful test on October 21, 1879, when it burned for thirteen and a half hours. It was not until 1880 that Edison patented a lamp that would burn for 1,200 hours using a carbonized bamboo filament.

It is thought that the incandescent light bulb had more than twenty inventors, but it is Edison who is primarily remembered for this accomplishment because he also provided a means to generate the electricity and deliver it to ordinary homes and businesses. He was also able to find a way to measure consumption so that users could be charged for the amount of electricity they used—thus making incandescent lighting economically viable.

On New Year's Eve in 1879, Edison strung up a two-wire system in Menlo Park, New Jersey, and illuminated the street. It must have been an amazing sight for those who witnessed it for the first time, but this was really just a baby step. For his first full-scale project, Edison chose a rundown warehouse on Pearl Street in the Wall Street financial district of New York City. He reportedly chose this location because there was a high density of customers in this very small area.

The Pearl Street generating station became operational in September 1882 and was a direct current system. It is interesting to know that Edison's metering devices were not ready for use when the station went on line, and customers received free electricity for the first six months or so.

Eventually, Edison owned companies that made light bulbs, built generators and other equipment such as meters, and constructed municipal lighting systems around the country. He founded Edison General Electric in 1889, which merged with the Thomson-Houston Company in 1892 to form General Electric, which is still in business.

A great conflict developed between Edison and his championing of Direct Current, and the followers of Nikola Tesla, who had pioneered the use of alternating current (AC). AC had the advantage over direct current (DC) of having the capacity to be transmitted over long distances without significant loss of voltage. Tesla partnered with George Westinghouse, and together they were advocating the use of AC rather than DC, which was strongly favored by Edison.

Edison claimed that AC current was dangerous and not in the public interest. As grotesque as it sounds, Edison tried to prove his point by using AC current to electrocute small animals and even an elephant named "Topsy." He called electrocution "being Westinghoused," and he and his workers invented the first electric chair at the behest of New York State for the execution of human prisoners.

Inevitably, AC electric current won out. When the first regional power station was built at Niagara Falls, New York, it was Tesla's alternating current system that was used. Power from the generators at Niagara Falls went on line November 16, 1896, and initially powered the industries that were located in nearby Buffalo, New York. As time passed, even Thomas Edison found himself in the business of producing equipment for AC power generation.

In a fairly short period of time, electricity became relatively commonplace in urban businesses and homes. When the lines came into homes, they ushered in more than electric lights. They also brought in appliances such as toasters, mixers, waffle makers, electric sewing machines, refrigerators, washing machines, ranges and ovens, and a plethora of other modern "labor-saving devices." In actuality, these machines did not save much labor, but they certainly made life more varied and interesting.

In this book we will be discussing some of these modern marvels—particularly those that are of interest to a wide spectrum of collectors. We will concentrate on the areas where the strongest collector interest seems to be—namely small kitchen appliances such as toasters, waffle makers, coffee sets, and mixers; fans; typewriters; electric lighting; phonographs; radios; and televisions.

Like the others in this series, this book will be patterned after the popular column "What is it? What is it worth?" which is found monthly in *Country Living* magazine. We will be spotlighting individual items in various categories, and each will be accompanied by a photograph, which will then be followed by a description of the item illustrated. Next, there will be a discussion of the item's origins and history plus relevant side notes under the heading "What is it?"

This will then be followed by the value under the title, "What is it worth?" Although this seems simple enough at first glance, it can be rather complicated. The central notion to keep in mind is that antiques, collectibles, and works of art have more than one value. For the purpose of this book, we need to explain two of these values—specifically, the value an object has when it is going to be insured and the much different value it has when it is sold.

Most of the prices we will be using are "insurance replacement values," which should be defined as the amount of money it would take for a private individual to go out and replace an item if it were lost, stolen, or destroyed. In other words, the "insurance replacement value" is what it would take for the owner of an object to go out and find a comparable replacement item and purchase it from a retail source in an appropriate marketplace within a reasonable amount of time.

Since most of us deal with the concept of a retail price every day when we go to the grocery or department store, it is probably easiest to think of the "insurance replacement value" as being the "retail" value. It is most important to remember, however, that this value is not the amount of money that an individual can expect to receive if he or she were to sell a similar item.

This standard is called the "fair market value" and is defined by the Internal Revenue Service as "the price that property would sell for on the open market between a willing buyer and a willing seller, with neither being required to act, and both having reasonable knowledge of the relevant facts." If the "insurance replacement value" is thought of as being "retail," the "fair market value" can be thought of as being "wholesale," and is generally 30 to 60 percent less than the "insurance replacement value."

As mentioned earlier, most of the prices in this book will be "insurance replacement value" or "retail," but occasionally, we will quote a price derived from an auction source, and these values are generally thought of as being "fair market value." It is true that the vast majority of all run-of-the-mill objects sold at auction do bring a "fair market value." But in recent years, auctions across the nation and around the world have increasingly become outlets for very rare items that sell for sums that are closer to or even above what might be considered the "insurance replacement value" before the sale took place and the "astounding" price was achieved.

Therefore, prices achieved at auction are open to interpretation, with some being "fair market value" and others closer to "insurance replacement value"—or even above. We remember being at an estate auction when a set of six mediocre Victorian side chairs made from walnut brought $5,000, to everybody's consternation. We were sitting close enough to the auctioneer to hear him turn to his secretary and whisper, "Now there is a world-record price that will stand for a thousand years!"

Achieving record prices does happen with some frequency, and whether an auction price fetched by a particular item is "wholesale" or "retail" depends on a number of factors, but the most important of these are rarity, desirability to collectors, and condition. Aside from these considerations, prices realized at auction that are significantly above "fair market value" might be the result of two or more bidders getting into an inexplicable "fight to the death."

We have seen buyers just hold up their numbered bidding placards at an auction and not take them down until the item being sold was theirs no matter what the eventual price. This "I will have it at any price" attitude tends to inflate prices dramatically because angry under-bidders sometimes bid the item up just to spite the eventual winning bidder as punishment for his or her uncompromising attitude.

Higher-than-normal prices can be realized at estate auctions when two or more members of a family decide that they are going to compete for the same object no matter what the cost. We remember watching a family squabble over an 1830s Chippendale-style chest that at the time had a fair market value of around $4,500. After long and acrimonious bidding back and forth, the piece sold for $29,000 because the various members of the family were determined to own the cherished heirloom without considering the eventual cost.

In this book, most of the prices will be insurance replacement values. These figures are our opinion based on market data research on the sales of similar items that were sold in similar circumstances. Prices derived from auction sources will be clearly identified, and whether that price is fair market value or insurance replacement value is open to some conjecture, but most often it will be fair market value.

At this point, we want to explore the various categories that we will be including in this book and discuss some historical background information. We will begin with the sewing machine, the invention of which preceded most of the other devices that we will be discussing by at least seventy-five years.

SEWING MACHINES

During the mid- to late eighteenth century, the Industrial Revolution made the looming of cloth much quicker and easier, and as a result, fabric became much cheaper. To take full commercial advantage of these textiles, a new machine was needed that could sew pieces of cloth together to produce affordable garments and other usable items. Such a machine would also be useful for stitching together pieces of leather to make such things as shoes and other sundry items.

In fact, the first "sewing machine" was designed to sew together pieces of leather to make footwear. It was patented by Englishman Thomas Saint in 1790 and used an awl to punch holes and a forked needle to pass the thread through the hole and make a chain stitch. Interestingly, Saint never made a model of his invention. His idea just moldered in the patent office until 1873, when Newton Wilson stumbled on the patent papers and decided to build a model, which he discovered would not work without some modifications.

Throughout the early nineteenth century, inventors tried to create a sewing machine. Many of these were for specialized purposes, and most tried to make a machine based on the way the human hand sewed—which was an impossible task. The first sewing machine used for commercial purposes was invented by French tailor Barthelemy Thimonnier, who patented his machine in 1830 and eventually had eighty of them working in his tailor shop in Paris.

The machines were expensive to make and they sewed only about 200 stitches per minute, but Thimonnier used them successfully to make uniforms for the French army. This so enraged the Parisian tailors, who were afraid for their livelihood, that they attacked Thimonnier's establishment and destroyed all of his sewing machines.

In the United States, the first practical sewing machine was reportedly made about 1834 by inventor Walter Hunt. He abandoned the idea of trying to invent a machine that would replicate hand stitching and went to a lock stitch that was easier for a mechanical device to produce.

Hunt's invention was not successful, and the actual "invention" and commercialization of the sewing machine were left to such men as Elias Howe Jr. and Isaac Merrit Singer. Howe is usually credited with inventing the sewing machine, but as we have discussed, there were a number of other patents before his.

In the early 1840s, Howe married and had three children. He was also lame and suffered from general ill health. Howe was a journeyman machinist in Boston, Massachusetts, and needed money badly, so he decided to get it by inventing a sewing machine.

After years of painstaking work, Howe came up with a practical sewing machine and challenged five seamstresses to a "sew-off." Howe's machine produced five seams before the human hands could produce one. Howe had a patent model by 1846, but unfortunately, each machine had to be individually hand crafted and, therefore, was very expensive to manufacture.

There were also no interchangeable replacement parts, and Howe's invention never received much commercial success.

That would be left to Isaac Merritt Singer, who started his professional career as a Shakespearian actor. In his earlier years, Singer had been an apprentice machinist, and he often supported his acting career with periods of working in machine shops and inventing gadgets such as a horse-powered drilling machine.

In 1850, Singer and his backer, George B. Zieber, were working in a machine shop that manufactured a type of sewing machine that was always breaking down and in need of repair. The owner of the machine shop asked Singer to improve the machine, and according to Singer, it took him just eleven days of intense work to significantly improve the apparatus being manufactured by his employer. As a result, Singer produced a patent model of his sewing machine in 1851.

Singer wanted to name his new improved device poetically after the "Swedish Nightingale," singer and actress Jenny Lind, but instead it became more prosaically known as the "Singer Sewing Machine." Interestingly, the new machine sold for around $125, which was a great deal of money in the mid-nineteenth century. Singer, however, toured the country promising dramatic recitations and mechanical wonders, and his company became the leader in the burgeoning sewing machine industry.

TYPEWRITERS

It took a number of centuries to go from Johann Gutenberg's movable type to the typewriter, but it is thought that the first mechanical device designed to imprint letters of the alphabet on a piece of paper to replicate writing was made by an Englishman named Henry Mills. The date was 1714, and all that remains of this device are some patent papers.

Yes, we know that this machine predates the sewing machine, which we describe as being the "earliest" apparatus we would be discussing. However, a practical typewriter did not really appear until the late 1860s and early 1870s, long after the sewing machine was fairly commonplace in American homes and businesses.

The first distant ancestor of the American typewriter, which made its debut in July 1829 was the "Typographer." It was invented by William Austin Burt and looked very much like a Federal period pinball machine with tapered legs and a clock-like dial on the front. Over the next fifty years, improvements were made in typewriting machines, dozens of patents were taken out, and all kinds of unusual mechanisms came into being.

If Charles Latham Sholes is considered to be the father of the American typewriter, he had a lot of help in gaining that distinction—namely that of Carlos Glidden, Samuel W. Shoule, Matthias Schwalbach, and James Densmore. One of Sholes' great contributions was the invention of the QWERTY keyboard, which is still in use today on computer keyboards despite numerous attempts to change or improve the arrangement of the alphabetical keys.

Sholes' patent on the typewriter was issued in 1867, but it took him until 1872 to decide that his new typewriting device was ready to be manufactured. He approached Philo Remington, who was president of the firearms manufacturer E. Remington & Sons of Ilion, New York. This meeting was the basis for establishing the Remington Typewriter Company that was to set the standard for the industry, and the Remington Model 1 first appeared in 1874. After this, many other famous names entered the mechanical typewriter business.

It is said by some that Thomas Edison invented the first electric typewriter in 1872 with his high-speed stock ticker. The first electric typewriter—as we understand it—was the model made by the Blickensderfer Manufacturing Company of Stamford, Connecticut, in 1902.

George C. Blickensderfer invented a manual typewriter in the 1880s and became a significant manufacturer of this type of machine. His 1902 electric typewriter was way ahead of its time, and today, only three are known to exist. At least one of these is said to be in working order still.

Most specialists say the first practical electric typewriter was invented in 1914 by James Fields Smathers of Kansas City, Missouri. While in the process of perfecting his machine, World War I intervened, and Smathers did not produce a successful model until 1920. The electric typewriter, however, did not really become popular with consumers until after the end of World War II.

PHONOGRAPHS

As was said earlier, one of the first things that Thomas Edison invented when he set up his workshops in Menlo Park, New Jersey, was the phonograph. Edison is purported to have invented the phonograph while working on two other devices—the telephone and the telegraph.

In 1877, Edison was trying to improve telegraphy by inventing a machine that would transcribe messages from a telegraph by making grooves on a paper tape, which could subsequently be sent over and over again on the telegraph lines. This led the great inventor to speculate that if he could do this with the dots and dashes of a telegraph message, why could he not do much the same thing with the spoken word transmitted over a telephone line? (In March 1876, Alexander Graham Bell had received a patent for a device that transmitted vocal or other sounds telegraphically.)

After some experimentation, Edison came up with an idea for using a diaphragm with a stylus that made indentions on moving paper as words were spoken. The paper was soon replaced with a foil covered cylinder and the phonograph was born. Edison had John Kreusi build the first phonograph machine based on Edison's ideas. When a person spoke into a mouthpiece, the sound vibrations were indented into the cylinder and could be played back later. The machine was successfully tested when Edison said, "Mary had a little lamb," into the gadget and the machine repeated the phrase back to him.

The phonograph was seen as a curiosity at first, and its development languished for a number of years while Edison toyed with other inventions. Then in the 1880s, Alexander Graham Bell got involved and improved Edison's invention primarily by using a wax cylinder to replace Edison's tin foil-covered version.

This new improved version of the phonograph had wider commercial applications than the original model, and Edison had great expectations for his invention. Edison envisioned the phonograph used in offices for dictation (steno machines). He thought of it being used in book publishing, and he foresaw its greatest purpose—the recording and dissemination of music. It took until the late 1880s, however, for the phonograph to begin realizing its commercial possibilities.

ELECTRIC FANS

Prior to the invention of electricity, fans used for cooling purposes were definitely low tech. Hand-powered fans have been around for thousands of years, and mechanical fans powered by servants pulling ropes to move a canvas-covered frame suspended from the ceiling date to at least the sixteenth century.

During the Industrial Revolution, fans in factories were often driven by belts that were powered by waterwheels, and in the late nineteenth century, fans were powered by fuels such as kerosene, alcohol, and oil. The electric cooling fan had to wait until Edison, Tesla, and Westinghouse made electricity in homes and offices possible.

The first fans were made for commercial establishments, not for homes. The electric ceiling fan was introduced in 1882 by Philip H. Diehl, who is considered by many to be the father of the modern electric fan. On the other hand, Dr. Schuyler Skatts Wheeler started developing the first personal desk fan in 1882, and his invention was sold by the firm of Crocker and Curtis.

Electric fans were very expensive until after the end of World War I, when the price of steel declined and industry began to be able to turn out mass-produced shapes for such things as fan blades. When prices declined, fans became more affordable for the average household and the number of fans used for cooling in homes proliferated greatly. Most of the household fans readily available to collectors tend to have been made from the 1920s to the 1960s, when central air conditioning made the electric fan somewhat (but not entirely) obsolete.

SMALL KITCHEN APPLIANCES AND OTHER HOUSEHOLD GADGETS

To reiterate, we will not be discussing full-sized kitchen ranges and refrigerators, but will concentrate on the smaller electric appliances that have become increasingly attractive to collectors.

When wires brought electric lighting to American homes, they also brought the possibility for a wide variety of other uses. To be sure, for a long time, electricity was limited to a few urban areas, but as it spread to cities, towns, and villages around the country, it became feasible for inventors and entrepreneurs to begin thinking about other ways to use this powerful commodity.

Fans and office equipment were at the forefront of this development. But by the early twentieth century, industry was beginning to think about other uses for electricity around the home. The result was a plethora of "labor-saving devices" which would theoretically "enrich" the life of the housewife/homeowner. Starting in earnest around the time of the end of World War I, all kinds of new products began appearing on the market that were made by such companies as General Electric, Westinghouse, Manning Bowman, Hotpoint, Sunbeam, Landers, Frary, & Clark (Universal) and others.

There was an outpouring of toasters, mixers, hot plates, coffee urns, waffle makers, popcorn poppers, and even table-side ranges. Many of these small appliances were not meant to be confined to the kitchen, but were intended to be used in the dining room next to the table. This placement facilitated the toast being fresh and hot and the coffee being at hand in its fancy percolator. It also allowed the art of waffle making to be demonstrated to family and guests, and to this end, pretty batter sets were made so that everything could be convenient and attractive in the dining room.

These appliances did not actually save much labor, but they did change the way people cooked and served meals—and the way they entertained. After the end of World War II, these devices became very common, and soon they were lined up on countertops across America like a regiment of metal and plastic soldiers.

RADIOS

An introduction to radio really takes us back to the telegraph (again). Originally, radio was actually called "wireless telegraphy." This terminology persisted in England until the mid-twentieth century with the radio being commonly referred to as the "wireless."

The operation of the radio receivers that we have in our homes and automobiles is based on radio waves, which are a form of electromagnetic radiation. This type of energy is created when an electron is accelerated within a frequency that is in the range called the "radio frequency" of the electromagnetic spectrum (a few tens of "hertz" to a few hundred "gigahertz"). For radio, this acceleration of electrons is caused by using alternating current in an antenna—but then again, most of us probably do not want to or need to know how our radios actually work. We just want them to work!

The theoretical foundation for the propagation of electromagnetic waves was laid in 1873 by Englishman James Clark Maxwell. In 1878, David E. Hughes was the first man to transmit and receive radio waves, but the scientific community dismissed his discovery as being a fluke and of no importance. Between 1886 and 1888, Heinrich Rudolph Hertz conducted experiments that validated the work of Maxwell, and radio waves became known as "Hertzian waves."

It should also be noted that in 1885, Thomas Edison took out a patent on a system that allowed radio communication between ships, and he subsequently sold the idea to Guglielmo Marconi. Who actually invented "the radio" depends upon whom you ask and how you phrase the inquiry, but the United States patent for the "wireless transmission" of data belongs to Nikola Tesla.

Many, many people played a role in the creation and development of radio—including Alexander Popov, Ernest Rutherford, and Roberto Landell de Moura—but we are most interested in the radio devices that began appearing in homes during the late first quarter of the twentieth century.

Wireless transmissions in Morse code were commonplace in the early twentieth century, but the idea of receiving spoken information and music in the home seemed like magic to the majority of people around the world. The first real radio broadcast occurred December 24, 1906, when Reginald Fessenden transmitted from Brant Rock, Massachusetts, readings from the Bible and played "O! Holy Night" on his violin. The world, however, had to wait until August 1920 for the first news broadcast on the radio, and the first regularly scheduled entertainment did not occur until 1922.

When radio stations began coming on the air in the 1920s, radios were fairly primitive and often homemade. Scientifically-minded children often built their own crystal sets which amazed their parents. Early radio receivers were battery powered, hard to tune, and had poor sound quality. Yet, if a family had one, the neighbors would come over and cluster around the unit just to hear the miracle that floated through the air. Radio became a national craze just as computers are today, and rooftops across the land sprouted antennas to catch the weak radio waves that passed through and around them.

It was something of a miracle. Invisible waves were being broadcast through the air and they carried an encoded signal that was picked up by an antenna. From the antenna, the signal, which was very weak, had to be amplified—or increased—by the radio receiver to the point where it was strong enough to operate the receiver's speakers. The speakers actually convert the electrical signal to sound waves, and we then hear (approximately) what was broadcast from the radio station.

It should be mentioned that early crystal sets did not have a power source and could not activate a speaker. The signals were weak, and the listener had to wear earphones to hear the atmosphere whispering to them.

Before we move on to discussing television, we want to emphasize one thing about collecting radios. If you happen across one in the marketplace, do not under any circumstances plug it in to see if it works. This simple act could destroy the radio within fifteen seconds and is a huge no-no! Just make sure that the case is in good condition and that all of the parts are there. Then, conduct a thorough examination to make sure that the application of electricity will not cause the set to short out or catch on fire. This may require the attention of a specialist.

TELEVISIONS

We think of television as a relatively modern phenomena because most of us were introduced to this device in the 1950s or later. Many people will be surprised to learn that the roots of television technology can be found in the nineteenth century. In 1885, Paul Nipkow invented a rotating scanning disk that would allow pictures to be transmitted over wires. This late nineteenth-century invention is considered the first electromechanical television system in the world.

Many people contributed to the invention of the television as we know it today. One of the most interesting was Philo T. Farnsworth (1906–1971), who is said to have gotten the concept of the electronic picture tube as a lad of just 14 (some sources say he was 13) while tilling a potato field outside Rigby, Idaho.

Farnsworth had a special interest in electricity and electrons. One day as he walked behind a horse going back and forth in rows, it occurred to him that an electron beam could scan images the same way. By age 21, young Farnsworth had a working device and many consider him the father of modern television.

Other people give this distinction to John Logie Baird, a Scottish scientist who gave the world's first public demonstration of mechanical television to members of the Royal Institution on January 23, 1926. Bell Laboratories also gave a public demonstration of television on April 7, 1926, by sending pictures and sound by wire from Washington, D.C., to New York City. In addition, a wireless demonstration was made over the twenty-two miles between Whippany, New Jersey, and New York City.

There were experimental broadcasts in the United States and Great Britain before the beginning of World War II, but they could be received only in specially equipped homes. It is interesting to note that several companies were advertising television sets as early as 1932—but few of us would recognize them as being the now-ubiquitous machine that snatches moving pictures out of the air or from a cable.

The first televisions were not the electronic devices that we know today. Instead, the screen, which was the size of a modern-day business card, had a motor with a spinning disk and a neon lamp that produced an indistinct, fuzzy reddish-orange picture that looked as if it were being transmitted from Mars.

Several of the devices looked like cathedral model radios with a small, round "porthole" at the top under the arch. A complete one of these, factory-wired with all the tubes and the neon lamp (yes, sometimes the consumer had to buy these separately), could cost as much as $120—which was a lot of money in the days just after the beginning of the Great Depression.

With most of these sets, owners were supposed to be able to listen to normal radio, plus police radio, ship-to-shore telephone calls, and what one advertisement called the "thrill of thrills," watching television. As one last side note, the first television commercial was broadcast in the United States in 1941.

MODERN AGE MISCELLANY

Finally, we will discuss a miscellany of "Modern Age" items that typify design in the mid-twentieth century. These will include cocktail shakers, bicycles, household implements, and accessories that exhibit what has been called "streamline design." Other items will be examples of what is often called "mid-century modernism."

We are mainly referring to objects made in the 1930s, '40s, and '50s. These objects have sleek, modern styling and can be found in every form, from kitchen appliances to office equipment. In general, these pieces are sleek, shiny, and streamlined—thus the name that has come to be associated with them.

The term "streamline" should be defined (in this case) as the paring down of forms into bullet and teardrop shapes that offer the least possible resistance to the flow of air or water. Sometimes, these pieces also exhibit parallel "speed lines" as part of the decorative motifs.

Henry Dreyfus, an important American industrial designer during this period, called streamlining "cleanlining." Streamlined objects appear to be light and suggest such ideas as speediness and sleekness.

Sewing Machines

Item 1

Grover and Baker Sewing Machine

Valued at $3,000

Sewing machine in a square mahogany box, which measures 13⅜ inches long, by 9¼ inches wide by 10¼ inches tall. Inside the case is a sewing machine with a brass plate that reads "Patent 11982, Feby. 11, 1851, June 22, 1852, May 27, 1854 and Howe's Sept 10, 1846." The piece is signed "Grover and Baker & Co," but the plate is worn and hard to read. The machine is in working order, but is missing the door on the case and only one hinge remains. There are additional minor wood losses to the case.

What is it? It is estimated that the Grover and Baker Company of Boston, Massachusetts, made more than 500,000 machines between the early 1850s and the time when they merged with the Domestic Sewing Machine Company in the 1870s. They made a wide variety of machines, including models for industry and models for home use, but they were pioneers in the field of the portable sewing machine, an example of which is pictured here.

Grover and Baker had the patent for the case that is shown with this machine, and the first examples came out around 1855. These are the first American portable machines, and they were made for a relatively long time. Grover and Baker made versions of this machine throughout the lifetime of the company, and the example shown here is the first configuration of these portable machines.

All the Grover and Baker portable machines produced a two-thread chain stitch, but the devices made in the 1850s are a bit different than the ones made in the 1860s, which are, in turn, different from the ones made in the 1870s. This first example is better made than the later machines, and the two urn-like posts that are seen on either side of the back of the sewing arm are not present on the later models.

This model is more frequently found than the second model, which first appeared in the early 1860s. It is estimated that fewer than 500 of the first Grover and Baker portable sewing machines have survived the past 150-plus years, but it is also reported that fewer than 100 each of the two later models are in existence.

What is it worth? The missing door and missing part on this particular machine impact the value somewhat. The insurance replacement value is $3,000 in this condition but in perfect condition might be $1,000 to $1,500 more.

Item 2
"Florence" Sewing Machine

Valued at $1,250

Sewing machine on an elaborate cast iron treadle stand. The stand has cabriole legs with pierced work in the rococo style. The pedals on this treadle stand are shaped like feet and have an openwork star in the heel. The top is walnut, and the machine itself is very distinctive looking with an elongated base terminating in a round platform. There is a little gilding on the machine and on one of the wheels of the treadle base. The machine is marked on the cloth plate.

What is it? This very distinctive machine is called the "Florence" because it was made in Florence, Massachusetts, by the Florence Sewing Machine Company. This company was the brainchild of Samuel Hill, who was one of the developers of Nonotuck Mill, which manufactured an improved silk thread.

Hill's involvement in making a stronger sewing thread probably led to his becoming interested in sewing machines after he saw one on display at New York City's Crystal Palace. The New York Crystal Palace was inspired by the London Crystal Palace Exhibition, which opened to worldwide acclaim in 1851. The New York version opened in 1853, and the original exhibition closed November 1, 1854. Other events were held there until it burned to the ground in 1857.

Hill reportedly saw the sewing machine at the Crystal Palace in 1855, and he opened the Florence Sewing Machine Company around 1860. At the time, it was the first large factory in the area that ran on steam power. The company went out of business in the late 1870s but was reopened by A.G. Mason in the 1880s as the Florence Machine Company.

There is evidence that at this time, the Florence Machine Company made machines for other companies, and examples made by them can be found with names such as "Crown," "Queen," and "New Queen." Sometime around the turn of the twentieth century, the company was moved to Cleveland, Ohio, and renamed the A.G. Mason Sewing Machine Company.

The Florence Sewing Machine Company moved into the popular culture of the day in 1870, when Thomas P. I. Magoun wrote the "Florence Sewing Machine Company Waltz." The sheet music for this ditty turns up in the ephemera marketplace from time to time.

The Florence sewing machine and treadle stand shown here are circa 1865, and this particular model is sometimes referred to as the "Fancy Florence." All Florence sewing machines were made to be used on a treadle base, but the company also made a mechanism that allowed the machine to be adapted for hand operation. This device had a double wheel crank that looks like it might have been removed from an old-fashioned store coffee grinder. It was mounted above the sewing machine and looks awkward to use.

Fancy Florence machines came with an elaborate, removable boxlike cover that is missing on this particular example. The surface of the piece shown here is relatively plain and unembellished. Some specimens have surfaces that are decorated with elaborate gold scrolling and reserves with very detailed representation of land-scapes and/or still-lifes depicting fruit and vegetables.

It is thought that the Florence Sewing Machine Company made more than 150,000 machines from the 1860s to late 1870s. What this means is that most of its sewing machines are not especially "rare," but the Fancy Florence is so attractive that enthusiasts really like having one in their collections.

What is it worth? The insurance replacement value of this Fancy Florence without its original cover is $1,250. With the cover, another $500 to $750 could be added. Florence sewing machines with really fancy decorations as described above are valued at around $500. One with the rare hand crank is very desirable and is priced at least $3,500.

Item 3
American Sewing Machine

Valued at $750

Sewing machine on four legs with floral painted base accented with much gold scrolling and the word "American" boldly written across the front of the base. The piece is cast iron painted black and is complete with its original shuttle. It is in very good working condition, and there is very little damage to the decoration.

What is it? There is really not a great deal known about the company that was responsible for manufacturing this interesting-looking machine. Even the founding date of this firm is open to some discussion.

There is no question that this company was located on Chestnut Street in Philadelphia, Pennsylvania, and was originally called The American Buttonhole, Overseaming, and Sewing Machine Company. Some say this firm was founded in 1869, but other more authoritative sources state that it was established two years earlier in 1867 and showed its product at the Paris International Exposition that same year.

Sometime in the 1870s, the company shortened its name to the "American Sewing Machine Company," staying in business until sometime in the mid 1890s (probably around 1895), and over the years offered a range of machines. Some had plain iron bases, but if someone wanted to go "whole hog," units with black walnut stands decorated with burl walnut or rosewood panels were available.

The appearance of the true American buttonhole machine is very distinctive. It has an arm that is decorated with openwork in a teardrop form and a treadle base. This machine is rather more valuable than the other American products, and one in good working condition has a retail value of around $3,000.

The American Sewing Machine Company apparatus shown here is circa 1875 and is a hand-crank table model of which American made a number of different versions. These came on a variety of bases, some rather fancy and others very plain. Some had just the embossed company name and the word "Patented," while others carried the embossed name of a local retailer who originally sold the machine.

What is it worth? The insurance replacement value of this American Sewing Machine Company piece is $750 in this condition.

Item 4
Wheeler and Wilson Sewing Machine

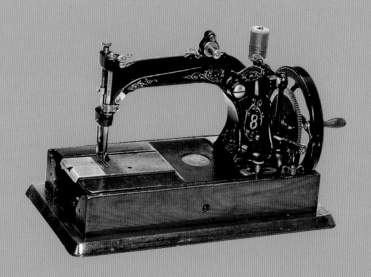

Valued at $350

Sewing machine, with raised "8" on the body and elaborate scrolling on the black surface. There is a gold medallion in the center of the base that has conjoined "Ws" and a 44 Union Square, New York City, address. The machine is mounted on a wooden base, and there is a large flywheel located at the back.

What is it? The Wheeler and Wilson Company was established in 1851 (some sources say 1852) in Watertown, Connecticut, to make sewing machines primarily for home and family use. The founders were Allen B. Wilson and Nathaniel Wheeler.

Not much is written about Nathaniel Wheeler except that he was a businessman who had an interest in a number of enterprises around Bridgeport, Connecticut. He reportedly lived in a mansion on Golden Hill Street, but this residence was torn down in the 1950s to make room for the new Bridgeport city hall.

Wilson, on the other hand, came from somewhat humbler beginnings. He was born in Willett, New York, in 1824 and was apprenticed as a cabinetmaker. In 1846, while working as a journeyman furniture maker, he began trying to invent a sewing machine. Just three years later, he developed the rotary hook-and-bobbin combination. This mechanism was used instead of a shuttle and would later form the basis for Wheeler and Wilson sewing machines.

The rotary hook arrangement was also quieter and smoother than the devices being used on other contemporary machines. Wilson patented his invention in 1850 and in 1854 came up with a "four motion feed" that moved the fabric after every stitch. This discovery is still in use on sewing machines made today. Even though the company was founded in 1851, full-scale production did not begin until after 1856, when the company moved to Bridgeport, Connecticut, and was renamed the Wheeler and Wilson Manufacturing Company.

In the early days of the company's existence—the 1850s and '60s—their sewing machine was the most popular brand made in America. This lasted until the late 1860s, when the Singer "Model 12 New Family" machine began to move that company into the forefront. Singer acquired the company in 1905 and continued to make the Wheeler and Wilson model D-9 until sometime in the 1920s.

Many collectors do not realize just how many "old" sewing machines there are out there. Wheeler and Wilson, for example, had a plant with five acres of floor space in 1863. In 1871, it had a yearly production of almost 130,000 machines—but by 1876, the number had fallen slightly to around 110,000 units. This is a large number, and it must be considered in context with the hundreds of thousands of other machines being made by other large companies such as Singer, Home, Household, National, and Wilcox and Gibbs, to name only a few.

The Wheeler and Wilson Model 8 that is shown here was first made in 1876—the year of the American Centennial celebration—and continued to be made until the introduction of the Model 9 in 1888. The Model 8 was designed for "Family and Light Manufacturing," and it is most often found on a treadle base.

The portable Model 8 is somewhat more difficult to find and a bit more valuable than the examples with the treadle stand. It was made circa 1878 and is in excellent working condition.

What is it worth? The Wheeler and Wilson Model 8 mounted on the treadle stand should be valued for insurance purposes at $200. This portable version, however, is worth $350 because it is rarer.

Item 5

Wilcox and Gibbs
Sewing Machine

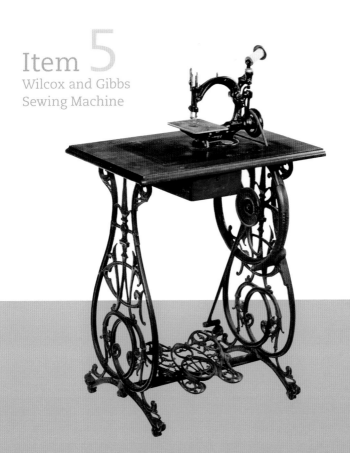

Valued at $300

Sewing machine painted black with gold
embellishments on a cast iron treadle
stand. This machine has its original
wooden cover, but it is not shown in this
photograph. The stand has conjoined
"W" and "G" initials on both vase-shaped
ends and on the foot-shaped pedals.
The machine is complete with its looper
and needle.

What is it? This machine is presented here because its appearance is striking and the treadle base is unusually attractive. However, one Web site we discovered declared it was not interested in machines by such makers as Singer (later full-size machines, not early or miniature ones), Wheeler and Wilson, Home, Graybar, Household, National, and Weed, among others. Many antique sewing machine dealers make it plain that they do not want to purchase old Wilcox and Gibbs machines because they were mass produced and are extremely plentiful. This opinion is echoed in many other places, and most sewing machines with these names are not especially valuable.

The Wilcox and Gibbs sewing machine has an interesting history that begins with James Edward Allen Gibbs, who was born in Rockbridge County, Virginia (in the Shenandoah Valley), in 1829. Over the years, Gibbs had a number of jobs including running a wool carding mill, but he was primarily a surveyor until he seriously injured his knee with an ax while cutting down a small tree.

With his injured joint, Gibbs was unable to return to surveying and he became a carpenter and a millwright. Gibbs is often listed as being a farmer, but he turned down his father-in-law's offer of 500 acres of land and the necessary equipment to establish such an enterprise. He did, however, become a farmer later in life.

In 1855, Gibbs happened to see a picture of a Grover and Baker sewing machine in an advertisement. Reportedly, it was the first time he had ever seen such a piece of equipment and he was curious as to how it worked. (Gibbs had already invented a device for carding wool more economically.) Unfortunately—or fortunately, as it turned out—the advertisement showed only the top part of the machine and not how the mechanism underneath worked using two threads to create a stitch.

Gibbs, however, decided that it was done using only one thread, and while he speculated on the supposed workings of the Grover and Baker, he formulated a way to produce a stitch with a single thread. Unbeknownst to him, he had just invented a completely new way for a sewing machine to work. This single-thread stitch is called a "chain stitch," and it was made using a rotating hook. He also became the only American inventor of a sewing machine who did not live in New England.

According to Anne Knox, in her article "James Edward Allen Gibbs" written for the *Virginia Cavalcade*, as the needle in the Gibbs machine descended through the cloth, the hook, which is located beneath the table or work plate, "formed the loop from the needle thread, and while the hook rotated, it held the loop open as the machine fed the cloth forward until the needle made the next descent through the loop held open by the hook. When the needle came down through that first loop, the point of the hook caught the thread to make a second loop, at which time the first loop was cast off and the second loop drawn through it, the first loop having been drawn up against the lower edge of the cloth to form a chain."

Gibbs did not appreciate the importance of his idea until he visited his father in Rockbridge County and went into a tailor's shop and saw a Singer sewing machine. To Gibbs, the Singer was too heavy, too complicated, too cumbersome, and much too expensive. This brought to mind his notion for a simpler, lighter, less expensive machine, and he began to try and develop it.

Gibbs worked on a model for his machine only at night and when it was raining because he had to work to support his family the rest of the time. He did not have the proper tools for the job, but he used his pocketknife to whittle a wooden model and, according to his daughter, used the root of mountain ivy to construct the revolving "looper" that was central to his innovation and invention. The revolutionary revolving looper is a device which pulled up a precise quantity of thread that was in proportion to the length of the stitch to be made by the machine.

Gibbs was a very bright man who realized that although he might invent a new sewing machine, he had no idea how to get it manufactured and marketed. Gibbs went to Philadelphia to find someone to help him. While he was sitting in someone else's office, James Wilcox came in, introduced himself, and told Gibbs that he dealt in inventions. He spirited the inventor away to his shop, where Gibbs built the requisite patent model of his machine, and on June 2, 1857, Gibbs received the official papers that detailed the invention and protected his rights as the inventor.

As a result, Wilcox and Gibbs formed a partnership, and J.R. Brown and Sharpe of Providence, Rhode Island, were chosen to produce the machine. For the rest of the mechanism used in their sewing machine, Wilcox and Gibbs had to pay royalties to Howe, Singer, and others, but with Gibbs' improvements, the resulting machine was small, quiet, and less expensive than competing models. In the late 1850s, a Wilcox and Gibbs sewing machine cost about half the price of other machines made by such industry leaders as Singer, Wheeler and Wilson, and Grover and Baker.

Sales of the Wilcox and Gibbs sewing machine began in 1858. The example that is seen here is a fairly standard model circa 1880. It is not readily apparent in this picture, but if viewed straight on, this machine has the configuration of a large G, and although other machines are constructed like this, many people say this G stands for Gibbs.

Machines such as this one are relatively common, but Wilcox and Gibbs pieces are important to the history of the development of the sewing machine. Gibbs' invention of the rotating hook to form a chain stitch is essentially still being used, and having an example with this seminal design is important to creating a comprehensive collection.

What is it worth? Despite the look and the age, this Wilcox and Gibbs machine has an insurance replacement value of just $300.

Item 6
Singer Featherweight Sewing Machine

Valued at $400

Portable sewing machine in its original carrying case, 15 inches long by 6 ¾ inches wide. "Singer" is stenciled on the sewing light, and "The Singer Manufacturing Co." is found on the back. This machine is in working condition, but the paint and gold trim show slight wear. Underneath the base is the serial number "AJ795124."

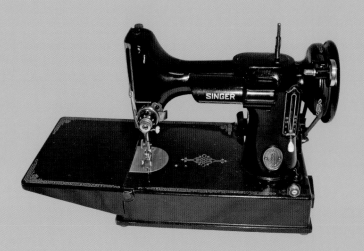

What is it? The history of the Singer Manufacturing Company is a long and distinguished one. In fact, the name Singer is almost synonymous with "sewing machine." We recounted the story of Isaac Merrit Singer and the founding of his company in 1851 in the introduction to this book. We will, however, very briefly explore some of the rarer and more valuable machines that this company made.

The Singer No. 1 was big and noisy, and it could be operated by hand or with a treadle. It is said that more than 10,000 of these were sold, but they are hard to find today because many of them were scrapped. The Singer No. 1 was manufactured until about 1860, when it was replaced by the Singer Model No. 2, which was actually produced until after the turn of the twentieth century.

Approximately 100,000 of this second Singer machine were made. They are available to dedicated collectors and have a very modest value on the current antiques and collectibles market. The No. 2 generally sells for less than $1,000, while the price of the Model No. 1 might exceed $12,000, depending on condition.

The first portable sewing machine introduced by Singer designed for home use is called the "Turtleback." It was made between 1858 and 1861, but only about 1,500 were sold because the machine was not powerful enough to sew on certain kinds of fabrics.

The Singer Turtleback has a big wheel, and the sewing arm was mounted on a base that looks something like a miniature butcher block table. These were usually elaborately painted and stenciled and can be found by themselves, on a treadle base, or in a wood and metal cabinet which can be extensively decorated. All Singer Turtlebacks that are in good condition are valuable, but the cabinet model can go into the $25,000 range depending on a number of variables.

Unfortunately, most Singer sewing machines which commonly turn up have very little value. A model that is more than 100 years old might sell for $200 or less. This is a little hard for many people to understand, but Singer was and is a very successful company and its later, full-size sewing machines are just not (for the most part) valuable.

One twentieth-century Singer sewing machine that is sought after and valued by both collectors and sewing enthusiasts is the "Featherweight." It is thought by many to be based somewhat on the "Sewhandy," which was made by the Standard Sewing Machine Company of Cleveland, Ohio.

The Singer Featherweight has an aluminum base and arm (the Sewhandy was largely cast iron), which makes it a truly lightweight portable machine that could be carried easily by just about anybody. The Featherweight also has a very characteristic flip-up extension table that provides a convenient work area for the operator.

The Featherweight Model 221 was introduced at the Chicago World's Fair in 1933, and an improved model came out in 1936. Singer Featherweight sewing machines can be found in black with gold accents, in beige/tan, and white/green. Any other colors signify that the machine has been repainted, and this constitutes a significant deduction in value.

The color of the Featherweight indicates (to some extent) where that particular machine was made. The black models were manufactured in Elizabethport, New Jersey, or Clydebank, Scotland. The beige and tan examples were made in Clydebank and St. John's Canada, while the white and green machines were made only in Clydebank.

Each Featherweight should have a serial number, which will give an approximation of the date of manufacture. The machine pictured here is serial number AJ795124, which signifies that it was made in Elizabethport, New Jersey, sometime between 1948 and 1950. For some reason that is not quite clear to us, some owners of Singer Featherweights want to know the actual "birthday" of their machine (are they planning a party?), and they can get some idea of what this date might be by calling Singer Customer Service at 1-800-4Singer.

There are several variations of the Model 221 Featherweight that are of interest to collectors, and generally, these examples command a bit more money than the standard model. There are, for example, the black crinkled paint and blackened parts (instead of chrome) models that were made during World War II, and the machines that were made for the Singer Centennial in 1951, which bear an oval seal to this effect.

Up until now, we have been discussing the standard Featherweight Model 221, but there was another model of Featherweight that is the most valuable of these machines. It is the Model 222 Singer Featherweight Freearm that was manufactured for only a short time because it was just too expensive to produce.

These relatively hard-to-find machines were first made in 1955 and can be distinguished from the regular models by the base, which is very different from the Model 221. This machine has a "freearm" and lowering "feed dogs" that allow the home seamstress to do freehand embroidery. This model was not sold in the United States but was marketed in Canada, England, Australia, and parts of Europe. Prices for the Model 222 Freearm start at about $1,000 for a machine in reasonably good condition and rise to around $1,500.

What is it worth? In this condition, the circa-1950 Singer Featherweight Model 221 has an insurance value of $400.

Item 7
Singer Miniature Sewing Machine

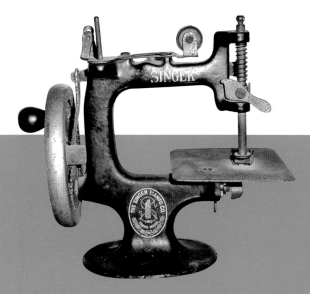

Valued at $125

Miniature sewing machine, approximately 6½ by 3 by 7 inches. The black frame is marked "SINGER" at the top and has an oval crest below which bears the representation of a bobbin with crossed needles surrounded by "The Singer Manfg. Co." above and "Trademark" below. The piece has seen a great deal of use, and there is pitting to the metal parts, but it is still in working condition.

What is it? The owner of this small Singer sewing machine is not sure whether it is a toy, a salesman's sample, or a real sewing machine. It was given to the owner's grandmother around the end of World War I, and she remembers the Singer salesman coming to the house to sell full-size sewing machines and bringing this miniature machine with him.

This particular machine is called the Singer Model 20. It came out in the early twentieth century, and a circa 1910 Singer advertisement clarifies its intended uses. First of all, the original price was $3, which was not altogether cheap in 1910 because this amount of money might have bought something like a week's worth of groceries for a small family.

The ad called this machine "Useful and Amusing" and described it as "a single thread sewing machine making an elastic chain stitch that does not unravel, if seam is locked as directed. It has no shuttle and no bobbins to be wound. There is no troublesome tension to be adjusted."

The copy goes on to explain that this machine was designed to be used by both "grown ups" and "little girls." It was presented as a simple sewing machine that would do a workman-like job and be useful during traveling. It was clearly stated that this machine could not do fancy work, but when it was clamped to a table or chair, would sew a straight line with great efficiency.

The advertisement said this machine was, for the young girl, "Not a toy but a Practical Singer Sewing Machine." The company also implied that this machine was a learning tool for little girls and a wonderful way for them to follow in "mommy's busy footsteps." It was claimed that any child over 4 years of age could use it and that "it is at once a fascinating amusement and a means of instruction in an essential household art."

One interesting variation of the Singer Model 20 was that it could be bought in a suitcase-like trunk with a beige background with red and white stripes, and this trunk also held a composition doll. There were pull-out drawers above and below the sewing machine compartment, where fabric and other sewing materials could be stored that would allow the little miss to work on her doll's clothes while she traveled with her parents.

Many other companies made miniature sewing machines comparable to the Singer models. In fact, Singer examples are probably the easiest to find, and collectors should look for models marked with such designations as "Spencer" (Spencer Sewing Machine

Company, Boston, Massachusetts) and "Little Nell" (E.A. Goodes), and some splendid round examples are titled "Pony," "Practical," and "Midget" (Foley & Williams, Kankakee, Illinois).

What is it worth?

This particular example is in rather rough condition and has an insurance replacement value of $125. If it were in better condition, that value would surpass $200.

Typewriters

Item 8
Odell Typewriter

Valued at $1,200

Machine marked on the cast iron base "Odell Type Writer Chicago, Ill." This designation is also found on a metal tag that has patent information. The base on the machine is circular and bisected by a roller to hold the paper. This is, in turn, crossed by a bar with numbers and letters. It is in excellent working condition.

What is it?

Mechanical typewriters are now virtually obsolete. They have been replaced by electronic devices that are far more forgiving of mistakes and make correcting errors much easier.

Few people familiar with mechanical typewriters and their standard keyboards would recognize the machine shown here as something that could be used to type a letter or create a document quickly and efficiently. But that is exactly what this device was designed to do and is an example of a special kind of typewriting machine that is called an index typewriter.

Index typewriters did not have keyboards per se, but instead had letters and numbers arranged along a straight or curved line or in a circle. To operate the machine, the typist (also called a "typewriter" in the early days) used one hand to operate a pointer that selected a character from the "index" of letters and numbers and depressed a lever with the other hand. This caused the character to be printed on a piece of paper.

The first successful index typewriter made in the United States was probably the Hall Type Writer, which was originally patented March 1, 1881. At the time, keyboard-style typewriters were rather massive and quite expensive. It was Thomas Hall's intention to create a lighter, more affordable machine with fewer moving parts.

He succeeded, and the three attributes listed above were the three major advantages of his and the other index typewriters that followed. Their major down side was that they were slow and did not print as well as the larger, heavier keyboard models. On the other hand, index typewriters were touted in contemporary advertising as portable machines to be used on trips and on railway cars.

Frank Eugene Odell was the inventor of the Odell Type Writer, which was first produced in 1889. The company's Model 1 had a straight base, but the five models that followed it had round bases similar to the one shown here. This machine was originally made by the Type Writer Company in Lake Geneva, Wisconsin, but the examples with the round bases were crafted at Momence, Illinois (Kankakee County near Chicago), by Odell, then by Odell-Young, and finally by the America Company. The last machine with the Odell name on it sold in 1906, and it was an Odell Model 5.

The machine pictured here is the Odell Model 2. It differs from the Odell 1b (the first round-base Odell) by the type of embossing on the round base. The 1b had a kind of large sunburst in the center surrounded by indented dots around the edge, while the Model 2 machines had "C" scrolls and stylized leaf motifs.

The other difference between the Model 1b and Model 2 is that the Model 2 is the first Odell machine where capital and lower case letters could be typed. The Model 2 does not have a model number on the base, but the later machines do have model designations— i.e. Models 3, 4, and 5.

The shifting from lower to upper case on the Odell Model 2 was accomplished by pressing a small lever that was mounted on the upper side of the type rail. The type was configured in two rows on a copper rail, and the characters were inked by an ink roll mounted on a spring.

As might be imagined, this was a difficult machine to operate, but an accomplished operator could generate up to forty words per minute. Truthfully, that must have been quite a feat of dexterity and concentration. It should also be mentioned that there was a check-writing attachment that could be bought as an accessory for the later Odell models.

What is it worth? This example of the Odell Model 2 has most of its original nickel finish on the cast iron base, and its value for insurance replacement purposes is $1,200. The Model 2 is one of the more available Odell index typewriters. The Model 1b is more than twice that figure, and the Model 4 is 50 percent higher.

Item 9
"Edison-Mimeograph" Typewriter

Valued at $8,500

Typewriter marked with the word "Edison" in bold caps with "Mimeograph Typewriter" below and "Made by A.B. Dick Company Chicago, U.S.A." Patent information is below that. The keyboard has seventy-eight characters, and the base is marked with two printings each of the words "Small," "Figure," and "Capital." There is a lever to the left and some gold scroll work below the ruler. This example is in good working condition.

What is it?

On August 8, 1876, Thomas Edison received a patent for "Automatic Printing," which detailed an electric pen used for making stencils and a flat-bed duplicating press for doing the actual printing. While working with waxed paper, Albert Blake Dick came up with a duplicating system, which he named the "Mimeograph," and Edison agreed to license his duplicating patents to Dick and help market the system as the "Edison-Mimeograph."

As the information on the machine indicates, it was Dick who invented the device shown for the express purpose of typing stencils to be used on the Mimeograph—but the machine could also perform other typing chores. Like the Odell mentioned previously, this is an index machine and a very clumsy one to use.

To work this typewriter, the operator rotated the large wheel at the base to select a character or figure—in lower or upper case. Each letter—upper or lower case or a figure—has a character on the type wheel. When one is selected, a lever that is seen jutting out on the left-hand side is depressed, allowing the printing to occur (the other lever was used for spacing).

Pressing the lever selects the character that is then raised by a tiny hammer and pressed against an inked ribbon. To complete the operation, the inked key makes contact with the paper or stencil held by the platen or roller.

As the keys move, they strike the paper on the underside of the platen, so this is an "understroke" machine, or a "blindwriter." This means the typist cannot see what has been typed unless he or she lifts the hinged carriage to see the finished work. In other words, it was very hard to establish any real speed on this typewriter, and any modern office typist would probably have thrown it out the window in sheer frustration within five minutes of trying to type a simple letter or document.

A company advertisement from 1894, however, touted the machine as, "A type-bar machine writing in perfect alignment permanently. Quality of work equal to the best. Durability unsurpassed. Simple in construction. Speed double that of handwriting."

Various dates for the first appearance of the Edison-Mimeograph can be found. They range from 1892 to 1895, but it is likely that this particular machine is circa 1894. The Edison-Mimeograph can be found in four models: the Model No. 1 has seventy-eight characters, and according to the 1894 advertising quoted above, cost $22. The Model No. 2 has eighty-six characters and also cost $22 in 1894. Finally, the Model 3 had ninety characters that allowed it to be adapted to typing in English, German, and French. This last model was a bit more expensive than the others at $25. The piece pictured here is the Model No. 1.

The Edison-Mimeograph typewriter manufactured by the A.B. Dick Company was on the market for only a short time. It has been reported that the other important makers of typewriters threatened office equipment suppliers with a boycott if they carried the Edison-Mimeograph. In response, Dick took the typewriter off the market to sell his Edison-Mimeograph Duplicator, which was a huge commercial success.

What is it worth? Since it was on the market for such a short time, the Edison-Mimeograph typewriter is very rare and valuable. Its insurance replacement value is $8,500 in this condition.

Item 10
"The Baltimore" Typewriter

Valued at $1,000

Manual typewriter in black case with "The Baltimore" stenciled across the front. It has a three-row keyboard. The machine is in excellent working condition, and the painted surface is also in good condition with only a few scratches and rubbed areas.

What is it? Early typewriters worked in a variety of ways, and this one is known as a "single element" machine. This type of device uses type-shuttles, type wheel, or type-sleeves rather than type-bars. On this particular model, a hammer moved forward from the rear and pushed the paper against the type. These "single-element" typewriters were cheaper than the "upstrike" models, and their type elements could be changed to permit the use of different fonts.

The history of this typewriter starts with the Munson Typewriter, which was patented by James Eugene Munson and Samuel John Siefried on September 17, 1889. This first Munson machine did not have a case per se to cover its working parts, but instead had a sleeve-like tube for the typing element.

This typing element was removable, interchangeable, and designed to allow the machine to be useful in foreign language applications. Weighing just 16 pounds, this remarkable machine was easily portable. The Munson Model 2 very quickly followed the Munson Model 1, and this new machine had an outer case to cover its working parts.

In 1897, the Munson Company was purchased by Edgar A. Hill of Chicago, Illinois, who called his firm the "Chicago Writing Machine Company." Hill began by producing the "Munson No. 3, but he quickly changed that name to "The Chicago No. 3." By early in the twentieth century these typewriters were just called "The Chicago."

Many may be wondering why The Chicago is being discussed when the machine pictured here is clearly marked The Baltimore. The reason is that these machines were actually sold under a variety of different names and one of these was The Baltimore. Sears and Roebuck marketed them as "Draper" typewriters, and they can be found with other names as well.

In 1902, the Chicago Writing Machine Company advertised that it had sold 26,000 of these machines since they were introduced in 1899. In 1914, their advertisements claimed that there were 75,000 of The Chicago type machines in service. Still, these machines are considered rather hard to find.

What is it worth? The machine shown here is early twentieth century (circa 1902) and is valued at $1,000 for insurance purposes.

Item 11
Underwood #5 Typewriter

What is it? Starting in 1874, the Underwood family made supplies for typewriters including ribbons and carbon paper. They supplied these items to the Remington Typewriter Company until that company decided to start manufacturing its own ribbons. Reportedly, this so infuriated the Underwoods that they decided to start making their own typewriters.

Franz X. Wagner invented a typewriter and showed it to John T. Underwood, who bought the company to get into the business. The first Underwood models appeared in 1895, but their models 1 and 2 are marked "Wagner Typewriting Company." In late 1900 or early 1901, the Underwood Model 5 came onto the market and became the company's most popular machine. Today, when many collectors think old typewriter, this is the device they have in mind.

Valued at $125

Manual typewriter marked "Underwood" with "No. 5" below the space bar. There are stenciled decorations around the body, and the sides are open, showing the internal workings. On the lower back, there is a long list of patent dates, the last one being May 1917. This particular example is in fair condition with wear to the stenciling and some scratches. The mechanism itself is in need of cleaning.

The Model 5 typed 84 characters and was a "frontstroke" machine, which allowed the typist to see what was being typed. This was something of an innovation that typists liked because most machines of the day were "understroke" machines, meaning the keys hit the paper on the underside of the platen.

These were called "blindwriters," because when the typist wanted to see what had been typed, work had to stop and the carriage had to be raised. On the Underwood Model 5, the keys hit the platen on the front—thus the term frontstroke—and the results were clearly visible without having to move anything.

All in all, the Model 5 was a superb machine; and by 1931, the serial numbers were approaching the 4 million mark. Today, these machines are extremely common, and large numbers are found in attics every day. Still, the popularity of these machines makes them saleable in the current antiques market.

What is it worth? Since this machine is in "as found" condition, the insurance replacement value is $125. Note: One very disturbing development we think we should mention. It has come to our attention that large numbers of old typewriters—such as the Underwood Model 5 shown here—are being bought on Internet auction sites, and instead of shipping the entire machine, the buyer requests that the seller cut off the keys and send only those. The keys are generally used to make jewelry—especially cuff links—and we are more than a bit appalled by this practice. To be sure, these machines are not rare items at the present moment, but to destroy them seems to be a bit like shooting passenger pigeons for sport. There may be lots of them now, but if too many are destroyed by having their keys removed, they too might become "extinct."

Related item

Manual typewriter with "The Smith Premier
Typewriter" stenciled on the top front bar in
front of the platen. This machine has two sets of
keys, one white and the other black. The black metal framework is open
on the sides and back and is accented around the base with nickel-plated
decorative reserves. The surface has significant paint loss and scratches.

What is it?
The Smith Premier Typewriter is an example of an upstroke blindwriter that
was mentioned in conjunction with the Underwood Model 5. The inventor
was Alexander Brown, an engineer who worked for the L.C. Smith &
Brothers gun manufacturing company in Syracuse, New York.

When Brown visited the American Centennial Exposition in 1876, he saw
the Sholes and Glidden typewriter and thought he could produce a better
model. Brown's employer gave him a place to work in the gun factory, and
work on the improvements began. Unfortunately, the task was a hard one,
and the Smith Premier No. 1 was not introduced until 1889.

Besides the mechanical upgrades, the new machine was quite attractive
and was decorated with images of cattails and flowers in relief around the
base. This was a double keyboard typewriter which used cranks and rods
that could be adjusted to make for a lighter touch. On this double keyboard,
each character had a separate key. In other words, there was a key for a
lowercase letter and another key for the uppercase of that letter and the
operator did not have to operate a shift key to produce a capital letter.

Another improvement was that the dried-on ink that crusted on the keys on
most other typewriters was more easily cleaned away on the Smith Premier
No. 1. The company advertising read: "All type cleaned in 10 seconds,
without soiling the hands, the use of a 'Toothbrush' not required." In fact, a
brush was required on the Smith Premier, but it was circular and mounted
inside the machine to make for a kind of "self-cleaning" device. In addition,
the platen knob on the Smith Premier could rotate the platen upward so
that the typist could see what had been typed. This was not a great
system, but it was an improvement over other "upstroke blindwriters." The
Model 2 Smith Premier came along in 1894, but it did not have the
decorative panels that are so distinctive on the Model 1 machines.

In 1903, the Smith Premier Typewriter Company changed its name to the
L.C. Smith & Brothers Typewriter Company. A few years later in 1906, the
Rose Typewriter Company introduced the first truly portable typewriter, and
in 1909, it changed its name to the Standard Typewriter Company. Its
"Corona" model typewriter was so successful that it changed its name in
1914 to the Corona Typewriter Company. When Standard merged with L.C.
Smith Brothers in 1926, the firm became Smith-Corona.

What is it worth?
Due to its condition, this Smith Premier No. 1 should be valued for
insurance purposes at $300.

Phonographs

Item 12

Edison Standard Phonograph Model "A"

Valued at $800

Phonograph in a two-part oak case with brass latches. The machine has a crank, and a brass horn that fits into a device that is marked "Reproducer Licensed for use only on Edison phonographs sold by Nat'l Phono Co." Although the case may have been refinished, the machine is in good working order.

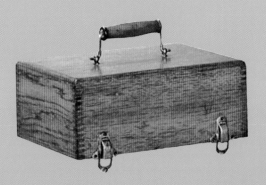

What is it? We discussed the early history of the phonograph in the introduction, but we can't resist including this story here. There is evidence that Edison did not construct his first phonograph until December 1877. Just before Christmas of that year, the intrepid inventor took the machine into *Scientific American* in New York City. He reportedly put the machine on a desk, turned a crank, and the device asked about everyone's health, said it was fine, then asked how everyone liked the phonograph, and finally bid everyone a pleasant "good night."

This created a stir, and the new invention was the subject of an article in *Scientific American* magazine plus several newspapers. This is said to have been Edison's favorite invention, and he might have thought that it was going to be an instant success—but it was not.

The Edison Speaking Phonograph Company was founded early the next year (1878), and the inventor and company namesake got $10,000 for the sales and manufacturing rights plus 20 percent of the profits. Unfortunately, the machine had problems. It was hard to operate and used a tin-foil-covered cylinder that produced an unsatisfactory sound. Consumers also viewed it as being something of a novelty rather than a product that they had to have in their homes.

The phonograph languished, and Edison concentrated on other things, but when Alexander Graham Bell and his cousin Chichester A. Bell along with Charles Sumner Tainter began making improvements to the phonograph, Edison's interest resurfaced. The Bells had come up with a new wax-covered cylinder and a stylus that floated rather than remaining rigid. The Bells approached Edison, seeking a collaboration, but Edison refused adamantly to join forces with his competition.

Edison went back to work on his phonograph, and he too came up with a wax cylinder to replace the old tin foil one. The Edison Phonograph Company was formed October 8, 1887, to market the new device. His "Improved Phonograph" was not introduced until May 1888, and it was followed shortly by the "Perfected Phonograph."

Again, things took a strange bounce when Jesse H. Lippincott took control of the several phonograph companies by purchasing the Edison Phonograph Company and becoming the sole licensee of the American Graphophone Company. Lippincott formed the North American Phonograph Company, but he saw the device as being primarily an office machine. Lippincott primarily leased phonographs to businesses to be used as dictating machines, but professional stenographers felt threatened by this machine and opposed its use strenuously.

In 1890, Lippincott fell ill and lost control of his company to Edison, who was the firm's main creditor. Edison changed the policy of the company from leasing to selling. But that is about all he did until 1894, when he declared bankruptcy for the North American Phonograph Company and subsequently bought back the rights to his invention.

Bankruptcy kept Edison from returning to the phonograph market until 1895, when he introduced the "Edison Spring Motor Phonograph." In 1896, he started the National Phonograph Company. Its emphasis was on the production of phonographs for home entertainment purposes instead of for business.

This new company was very successful, and within a few years had branches in Europe. In 1896, the company introduced the "Edison Home Phonograph" and also began to manufacture cylinders for use on these phonographs. In 1898, the "Edison Standard Phonograph" was introduced, and an example of this model is shown here.

The "Standard" or "New Standard," as it was sometimes called, was vigorously advertised as producing "the same results as the other famous models of the GENUINE EDISON PHONOGRAPH, using the same records, and the same reproducer. Simplest, most durable, and cheapest talking-machine." At $20 retail, this new machine was indeed inexpensive relative to other machines, which had sold for as much as $150 just a few years earlier in 1891. Prices kept falling, and in 1899, the "Gem" model phonograph sold for a mere $7.50.

The Standard Model was the first to carry the Edison trademark design, but it does not appear on the case shown here, which suggests that the oak case did not have it originally or that it may have been refinished. This machine used the standard two-minute cylinders and has the Model C reproducer.

What is it worth? With the horn and the Model C reproducer (which is worth about $175 by itself), this circa 1900 Edison Standard Model "A" is valued at $800.

Item 13
Columbia Graphophone

Valued at $1,800

Phonograph in an oak case.
The case has a scroll-type label
on the base that reads "The
Graphophone." There is a rope-
type edging around the top of the
lower portion of the case, and
the corners have raised vasiform
decorations. The piece with its
original horn is in good working
condition.

What is it? Earlier, we discussed the development of the Edison phonograph and briefly mentioned the improvements to Edison's machine made by Alexander Graham Bell and his team. Bell had won the 50,000-franc Volta prize from the French government for the invention of the telephone. He took the money and in 1880 established the Volta Laboratory in Washington, D.C. There, he worked with a team including his physicist cousin, Chichester Bell and model-maker Charles Sumner Tainter.

The Bell group worked on the problem of transmitting sound and sound reproduction and experimented with sound transmission using light beams and magnetic recordings. They also worked on sound reproduction using compressed air and jets of water— pretty advanced for the 1880s.

Their biggest success, however, was a little more prosaic. It came in 1881, when Bell and his associates found that they could store sound vibrations on a wax-covered cylinder, greatly improving the sound of the phonograph. This was a cardboard tube approximately 1 5/16 inches in diameter and 6 inches long. Its biggest drawback was that it was suitable only for a single use.

Another improvement made by Volta Laboratory was for an interchangeable floating head that recorded sounds by using a gravity-pressure stylus to incise grooves into a removable wax cylinder. This was a great improvement over the Edison method, which used a rigid, fixed stylus to record the sound.

The Volta Laboratory's machine, patented May 4, 1886, was given the name "Graphophone," which was a rearrangement of the letters in the phonograph to get around Edison's use of that designation. The Volta Graphophone Company was founded in 1886 to hold the patent and to do further research. The manufacturing and marketing arm, the American Graphophone Company, was not founded until May 1887.

Bell actually approached Edison to share the improvements, but the great inventor vehemently rejected the overture. Instead, Edison found a way to improve on the improvements by adopting the floating stylus. He added a motor and an improved solid wax cylinder (actually not made from wax, but from a kind of metallic soap).

Jesse Lippincott's North American Phonograph Company leased Edison's and Bell's phonographs for office purposes. Lippincott thought that some day, the phonograph would be as indispensable a piece of office equipment as the typewriter. In this arrangement, the Edison phonograph outsold the Graphophone by a wide margin because the Edison machine used a spring-driven motor, not a treadle the way the Graphophone did, and the Edison solid wax cylinders were better. American Graphophone's business began to dwindle, and by 1890, the plant in Bridgeport, Connecticut, was all but idle.

The only company that did well with the Graphophone was the Columbia Phonograph Company, which had a sales territory encompassing Washington, D.C., Maryland, and Delaware. This company found that these machines sold best when used to play prerecorded music.

At the time, mass production of musical cylinders was not possible. To get around this problem, Columbia, enjoying a relationship with the United States Marine Band, had the orchestra go into a studio several times a week and play. These sessions were recorded on a number of machines while the band performed.

This was president of Columbia Records Edward D. Easton's idea. He joined the board of American Graphophone, toured the country surveying the market, and found the consuming public preferred the improved Edison machine to the Graphophone.

With the collapse of North American Phonograph Company in 1894, Edison and Graphophone began to fight it out in the marketplace. Easton, who was now vice-president and general manager of Graphophone, sued many of the important individuals and companies in the phonograph business and threatened to sue anyone who bought or sold Edison phonographs.

In 1895, the business of the American Graphophone Company began to improve with the introduction of several spring-motor-driven phonographs. These included the Type F, the Type K, the "Baby Grand," and the Type N, which is said to have brought the phonograph into widespread use. The Type N had the advantage of costing just $40, and although this was still fairly expensive, it was affordable to most of the American middle class.

In late 1896, Edison and Columbia Graphophone arrived at a truce that called for a cross-licensing agreement. In 1896, Graphophone introduced the Type A, which, at $25, was even more affordable than the Type N of the previous year. This new model had a cast iron top mechanism instead of a more expensive nickel-plated and aluminum apparatus. The Type A also had a compact spring motor.

In 1897, the company expanded and moved to New York City from the old Volta Laboratory in Washington, D.C., which was too small for the burgeoning enterprise. Columbia Graphophone continued to prosper and offer new lines, and in 1901, it introduced the Type AA, which is shown here.

This is a small nickel-plated machine that plays standard-size cylinders. It has a motor based on the very popular Type B. The Type B was sometimes called the "Eagle" because it cost $10—or the same as a $10 gold piece, which had an eagle on it and was commonly referred to as an "eagle." It also has an eagle reproducer. While the Type B retailed for a modest $10, the Type AA was a bit more and originally retailed for around $18.

The same year this model was introduced, Columbia produced its first disc record player and began selling disc records. In 1908, it introduced double-sided disc records, and in July 1912, the company discontinued making cylinder recordings and cylinder phonographs. An era had ended.

Note the shape of the box on this Columbia Graphophone Type AA. It is a configuration that is associated with Graphophone and makes one of these machines identifiable at a distance without seeing the decal markings.

What is it worth? Insurance replacement for this Columbia Graphophone is $1,800.

Related item

This 39-inch-tall combination disc phonograph and music box is marked "Reginaphone" on the lid. The Regina music box has double combs, a zither attachment, and a short bedplate. There is a removable 10-inch turntable. The phonograph, made by the Columbia Phonograph Company, has a flower-shaped horn. The serpentine case is mahogany with paneled lid and storage drawer with ten discs.

What is it?

The invention of the phonograph was the beginning of the end of popularity for the music box. To be sure, many people still love the charming tinkle made by music boxes, but starting in the late nineteenth century, families could listen to more realistic music and hear the reproduction of human voices on the more modern invention.

In 1892, Gustav Brachausen, founder of Polyphon Musikwerke of Leipzig, Germany, came to the United States with three engineers and two cabinet makers to establish a company making high quality music boxes. He began manufacturing that same year, but the Regina Music Box Company was not actually incorporated in Jersey City, New Jersey, until 1894.

In 1896, it purchased land in Rahway, New Jersey, and moved production there. Unfortunately, by 1902, the sales of music boxes had begun to plummet and the company had to diversify. In that year, it became known as the Regina Company and began making home appliances including a hand-operated vacuum cleaner. Regina also entered into an agreement with the Columbia Phonograph Company to make phonograph parts for a device that was both a music box and a disc "talking machine." This was called the Reginaphone.

A 1910 advertisement for this machine reads: "A Talking Machine and Music Box Combined. Two Instruments in One. Real Music in Your Home." The ad went on to say, "It will play regular disc talking machine records, as well as Regina steel tune discs." To do this, the Reginaphone had a turntable, a horn, and a phonograph arm as well as a music box.

This particular Reginaphone has a short bedplate, which is characteristic of the company's later music boxes. The bedplate was about half the width of the case, which left a space below on the left side with a lower sound board. This arrangement allowed for an improved sound for the music box.

The most commonly found Reginaphones are table models with oak cases. This mahogany floor model with its undulating curved or serpentine lines is very attractive and hard to find. There is a plate on this piece with patent dates that go back to May 1899, which indicates that this machine was probably made in the early twentieth century.

What is it worth?

This Reginaphone sold at auction in 2006 for $7,638.

Item 14
RCA Portable Phonograph

Valued at $2,703

Portable phonograph with metal case, 8 inches high, with a width of 15½ inches and a length of 17¾ inches.

What is it? Today, the initials RCA are a brand name used by two different companies, one that produces consumer electronics and one that produces recordings. However, the history of the Radio Corporation of America—RCA—really begins during World War I, when the patents held by various American companies that dealt with radio technology were consolidated to serve the war effort better.

After the war, the U.S. Navy tried to organize American radio into a monopoly but failed. The U.S. Congress was convinced to entrust this role to General Electric working in concert with American Telephone and Telegraph (AT&T).

These two companies (along with others such as United Fruit and Westinghouse) formed a publicly held company in 1919 and dubbed it the Radio Corporation of America. This new company took over the assets of American Marconi and acquired the radio patents held by Westinghouse and United Fruit. The new company

also was responsible for marketing General Electric and Westing-house radio equipment.

By 1926, RCA had put together a network of radio stations, which they titled the National Broadcasting Company—better known today as NBC. In 1929, RCA purchased the Victor Talking Machine Company—maker of phonograph records and the famous "Victrola" phonograph—and the name of the company changed to RCA-Victor.

It should also be mentioned that RCA-Victor was responsible for developing the first 33 1/3 rpm (revolutions per minute) records in 1931, but the privations of the Great Depression initially made this type of format something of a commercial failure. In addition, RCA introduced the first 45 rpm records to the public in 1949.

The portable record player shown here, with its largely aluminum case, was manufactured in the mid-1930s and was much ahead of its time. The designer was John Vassos, who was born in Greece in 1898. From a very early age, he was artistically inclined and was a political cartoonist for a newspaper in Constantinople (now Istanbul), Turkey.

Unfortunately, the 16-year-old Vassos drew an unflattering picture of the Turkish Senate and was forced to flee for his life. He eventually arrived in the United States in 1919. He studied art in Boston under John Singer Sargent and designed stage sets for the Boston Opera Company.

He opened his own studio in New York City in 1924, where his art was used in window displays for Macy's Department Stores. He also produced advertising for clients such as General Tire. His strong, vibrant Art Deco images rejected the old Victorian and Edwardian styles.

Prior to the beginning of World War II, Vassos did book illustrations as well as more advertising work, but as the demand for lavishly illustrated books declined, he began to do industrial design projects for RCA. One of his most famous was for a television set in a clear Lucite cabinet. This object, featured at the 1939 New York World's Fair, was made in this transparent material to demonstrate that the pictures on the television screen were "snatched" from the air and not generated from inside the set itself.

Vassos worked for RCA for some forty years. In his early years, he designed this portable record player with its case that is made mostly from aluminum, which is the most abundant metal in the earth's crust. It was first separated from its ore in the 1820s and was considered a semiprecious metal—at one time, one ounce of pure aluminum cost twice the daily wage of the average worker, and it was even used to make fine jewelry. Then, in 1886, a cheaper way to extract the metal from bauxite by using electricity was discovered, and aluminum became more available for a variety of uses.

In the 1930s, when this portable record player was produced, aluminum was still something of an exotic metal and would not become commonplace until after cheap sources of electric power provided by hydroelectric dams entered the equation. In any event, Vassos probably chose aluminum for his record player because it was exotic and had a very distinctive silvery surface.

This metal was also appropriate because it was lightweight and, therefore, suitable for a portable object that otherwise might be unwieldy. Aluminum is also corrosion resistant, which might have been seen as a plus for a device designed for use indoors and on porches and patios.

What is it worth? This piece sold at auction for $2,703.

Electric Fans

Item 15

Edison Manufacturing Company Fan

Valued at $10,575

Desk fan with six brass fan blades, each of which is stamped "Edison Mfg. Co." It has twin terminals, with an enclosed motor, and an additional mark on the tripod base. It is 10 inches high, and there is no cage over the blades.

What is it?

Concrete information about the fan shown here is scarce, and what is available are just a few scattered brief mentions and some extremely vague clues. Thomas Edison is responsible for so many inventions and founded so many companies to exploit those inventions that it is sometimes very difficult to trace his business activities with any clarity.

Edison became interested in making pictures move in 1888, when the famous English photographer Eadweard Muybridge visited him in West Orange, New Jersey. Almost immediately, Edison started trying to invent a motion picture camera and projector. The result of his work was the "Kinetograph," a motion picture camera, and the "Kinetoscope," a motion picture viewer.

The name of this latter invention was derived from the Greek words "kineto," or "movements," and "scopos," to watch. These were so-called "peep-hole" viewers, which allowed only one person at a time to view the action. Edison founded the Edison Manufacturing Company in 1889 (it became Thomas A. Edison Inc. around the turn of the twentieth century), and its main purpose was to manufacture the Kinetograph, the Kinetoscope, and to make motion pictures.

Most if not all of these pictures were called "Actualities," meaning that they dealt with news events, famous people, disasters, expositions, scenic views, and the like. Now, what does all of this have to do with the fan shown here? Well, in Edison's papers, there is a notation that he was also using the Edison Manufacturing Company to make batteries that could be used in conjunction with the phonograph and to operate such things as railroad signals and cigar lighters (an odd grouping to say the very least).

The same papers note that the company had developed a successful fan motor, and our information is that this fan could be operated on batteries. It was called the "Iron Clad" fan and was a fairly small desk fan with blades that were fully enclosed in an iron surround. This feature is missing on the fan shown here, but despite this loss, this fan is very hard to find and of great interest to many collectors.

What is it worth?

This very rare fan sold at auction for $10,575.

Item 16
Westinghouse Fan

Valued at
$200

Small electric fan with four blades, approximately 14½ inches tall; the diameter of the blade guard is 11 inches, and the blades are 10 inches across. The front of the blade guard has a circular insignia with a large "W" above "Westinghouse Electric" in a cartouche. On the motor housing, there is a tag with patent dates, the last one being 2-29-15. This plate also notes that this is a style 241853A fan. There is a sliding speed control on the base. The fan is in working condition and appears to have its original cord.

What is it? George Westinghouse was born in Central Bridge, New York, in 1846, the son of a factory owner in Schenectady, New York. It was there that young George learned about mechanics and manufacturing. At 15, he fought for the Union during the Civil War, and after the conflict was over, he studied engineering at Union College.

Westinghouse began to formulate ideas for inventions, most of which had to do with railroads. At the time, the safety record of the railroad was horrific—unthinkable by today's standards. His first big contribution was a compressed-air brake system that could be efficiently operated by the train's engineer rather than having to go through the "brakeman."

In 1868, Westinghouse established the Westinghouse Air Brake Company in Pittsburgh, Pennsylvania. It was this invention that made Westinghouse a successful and wealthy man. His position was greatly improved when Congress passed the U.S. Railroad Safety Appliance Act in 1893, which made air brakes mandatory on all trains.

Westinghouse's interests were far ranging and included such things as inventing improvements for oil exploration and the growing telephone system. In the 1870s, Westinghouse was a big name in American industry while Thomas Edison was still just a struggling inventor with a few fairly unheralded successes to his credit.

When Edison first supplied electricity to fifty-nine customers from his Pearl Street station, Westinghouse investigated and came to the conclusion that Edison's system was too inefficient for distribution over large areas. Edison used low-voltage direct current (DC), but around 1885, Westinghouse began experimenting in Pittsburgh with the distribution of alternating current (AC).

Westinghouse with partners William Stanley and Franklin Leonard Pope refined the AC distribution system and in 1886, installed the first multiple-voltage AC power system in Great Barrington, Massachusetts. Unfortunately, this system was dangerous if not properly designed and used, and Pope was actually electrocuted by a malfunctioning AC converter.

In 1886, the Westinghouse Electric & Manufacturing Company was founded, but the name would change to Westinghouse Electric Corporation just a few years later in 1889. What Westinghouse needed was a meter to gauge how much AC power was being used and a motor that used AC power for its operation.

Nikola Tesla invented an AC motor for Thomas Edison. Then the two men had a serious falling out over money, and Westinghouse obtained the rights to Tesla's motor. Using Tesla as a consultant, Westinghouse expanded his electrical empire, and in 1889, the company produced its first electric desk fan.

By 1905, Westinghouse had perfected an alternating current fan motor with an internal on/off switch, which was called a "tank" motor because of its large size and shape. The company introduced its first vane oscillating fan in 1909, and in 1912, it came out with a mechanical oscillating fan that was the best of its kind.

Early Westinghouse fans tended to have heavy cast iron motor housings and cast iron bases with heavy-sheet brass blades. The cage over the blades usually had the characteristic S shape and was made of brass as well. Early Westinghouse fans also tended to have 12-inch blades,

The fan shown here has nickel-plated brass blades and an unusual straight wire or "spoke" blade guard or cage instead of the more typical one with S-shaped wires that visually suggested a blowing breeze. It is an oscillating fan, and the Westinghouse badge found on the front of the blade guard on this model suggests that it was probably made sometime between 1919 and 1923.

What is it worth? The condition of this fan is good but not excellent, and its insurance replacement value is $200.

Item 17
Diehl Electric Fan

Valued at $350

Large desk fan with a front medallion that reads "Diehl," approximately 17 inches tall with 12-inch brass blades. It has its original cloth-covered cord and a sliding speed control on the back. A tag indicates that this is style 1251 made by the Diehl Manufacturing Company of Elizabeth, New Jersey. There is some loss to the black enamel finish, and the brass blades are tarnished, but the fan is in working order.

What is it? Philip Diehl came to this country in 1868 and through hard work became something of a "big deal." Diehl was born in Germany in 1847, and upon arriving in the United States, he took a job with the Singer Sewing Machine Company. He almost lost his life in the great Chicago fire of 1871, after which he moved to Elizabeth, New Jersey, where he continued to work for Singer. He developed and improved Singer's sewing machine models. It was he who developed the first electric Singer sewing machine motor.

One of the most significant contributions made by Diehl was for a product that never made it into American homes on a commercial scale. In the early 1880s, Diehl developed an incandescent light bulb that had no lead-in wire and, therefore, could be patented in its own right in competition with Thomas Edison's incandescent light bulb. Edison had been charging stiff royalty fees to manufacturers who wanted to produce his light bulbs, and it is said that those who paid this fee actually faced bankruptcy. After Diehl secured his patents in 1882 and 1883, Westinghouse Electric bought the rights to the bulb for $25,000—a huge sum of money for the time.

Westinghouse then used Diehl patents to force Edison to lower the royalties and thus promote the manufacturing of electric lighting that was more affordable for the public to buy and profitable for manufacturers to produce. Diehl's light bulb was never manufactured on a commercial scale, but it did have a large impact on the availability of lighting in American homes. Today, Diehl incandescent light bulbs are rare and valuable.

In 1887, Diehl attached blades to the flat motor he had developed for the sewing machine and suspended it from the ceiling of his home, creating the first direct-drive ceiling fan. For clarity, it should be mentioned that the actual first ceiling fan created by Electro Dynamics in 1884 was battery powered. There was also a Hunter Brothers ceiling fan in 1886, but the one created by Diehl was the first to have a direct drive.

Diehl decided to market this fan, and along with three of his Singer co-workers, formed Diehl and Company to manufacture the ceiling fan. This fan was not actually patented until 1889, and shortly thereafter, he invented an electric light called an "electrolier" that attached to the ceiling fan. Diehl pioneered a number of different types of fans. He put a fan on a pole and sold it as a "column fan," and the company also made a crude desk fan. Some credit Diehl with making the first desk lamp.

In 1896, the name of the company was changed to Diehl Manufacturing, and in 1904, it developed a split ball joint that allowed the
fans to swing back and forth and be adjustable. Then, in 1907,
Philip Diehl's nephew, Frederick, invented a type of oscillating fan
which collectors refer to as the "walking foot." Later that same
year, the company developed another type of oscillating fan commonly referred to as a "C" frame. Other types of Diehl oscillating
fans are called "kidney oscillators" and "toilet bowl oscillators"
because of the shape of the backs of the fans.

Until 1914, Diehl had been working in part of the Singer Sewing
Machine compound in Elizabeth, New Jersey. In 1914, they built a
new factory, and in 1918, Singer took over Diehl Manufacturing.
Diehl became a division of Singer.

The Diehl oscillation fan shown here is circa 1914, and its heavy
cast iron body and motor housing are typical of fans Diehl made
before the end of World War I.

What is it worth? The insurance replacement value
of this Diehl fan is $350.

Small Kitchen Appliances and Other Household Gadgets

What is it? Many collectors consider this the ultimate in American toasters. It was reportedly manufactured between 1927 and 1929. (Although some say it was made as late as 1940, the 1927 to 1929 dates are from a preponderance of sources.) This pattern can be found in two color schemes: red (or pink) and blue, with the red being somewhat rarer.

The Pan Electric Manufacturing Company also made this same shaped toaster with a printed pattern of scattered flowers. This, like the "Willow" pattern pieces, is very rare. In addition, Pan Electric made Toastrite toasters without a transfer-printed decoration, and examples can be found in iridescent blue, apple green, mottled orange, yellow, and mother-of-pearl. These solid color examples have Rayo silk power cords in colors that match the surface of the toaster. Solid-color Toastrite toasters are much easier to find and somewhat less valuable than the examples with the Willow prints.

Valued at $4,000

Electric toaster with heating elements set in a ceramic framework decorated with an Asian-themed design, approximately 6¾ inches tall and 8¼ inches wide. There is a long trough-like groove on either side of the toaster to hold slices of bread. It is marked "Toastrite 110 Volts 500 Watts The Pan Electric Mfg. Company Cleveland, O." It is in good working order with original cord and no chips or cracks.

The print found on this toaster appears to be Chinese but actually has very little connection to the legends of China. In the Western world during the eighteenth and nineteenth centuries, Chinese art and design were very popular, and a large amount of Chinese porcelain was imported into Great Britain, Europe, and the United States at great expense.

In the eighteenth century, English manufacturers started imitating Chinese motifs on pottery and porcelain because these items sold quickly. Manufacturers came up with a lot of Asian-looking patterns, but starting in the early nineteenth century, they began producing a variety of designs featuring a large willow tree, plus combinations of other motifs that included water, a boat or boats, a bridge, a pagoda or pagodas, human figures, and sometimes birds.

Today's collectors know these patterns as Willow, or Blue Willow, characterized by dark blue pigments common to the nineteenth century. These images are supposedly based on a Chinese story, but that is pure invention designed to sell the product.

The story goes that an emperor named Tso Ling (no such ruler existed) had a daughter named Kwang-se or Koong Shee. She fell in love with Chang, her father's clerk or accountant. The emperor, however, had pledged his daughter to a rich, elderly merchant and exiled Chang while sending his daughter to live in a blue house.

Chang broke into the compound and he and Kwang-se eloped, fleeing over the bridge while pursued by her father, who wants to execute them for their disobedience. As they reach the crest of the bridge, the gods take pity on their plight and transform the lovers into a pair of doves, which are shown "kissing" with their beaks together in the air over the bridge.

Since the pattern was first used in the early nineteenth century, many manufacturers in England, Japan, and the United States have made versions of this legend, and it is very popular with current collectors. An adaptation of the legend was used by the Pan Electric Manufacturing Company so that the toaster would match the Willow ware dishes that were being used at many breakfast tables.

Toasters such as this one are often referred to as being "porcelain" or "porcelain front" toasters, but this particular type was not made from true porcelain. Instead, it was made from a heat-resistant ceramic called "onyxide" that is more closely related to ironstone than it is to the type of porcelain from which fine china is made.

Toasters such as the one on page 70 are sometimes called "perchers" because the bread was meant to be perched in the groove that ran down either side of the toaster. The bread was slid into the long slot, and when the side that faced the heating elements was toasted to the taste of the diner, the piece could be pushed out and turned over or eaten the way it was.

What is it worth? The solid-color version of this Toastrite toaster has an insurance replacement value of $1,600. One of the Pan Electric Pink Willow toasters, which is somewhat rarer than the blue version, recently sold at auction for $6,400. A Toastrite toaster with a scattered floral decoration sold on eBay in 2002 for $6,331. At the current moment, the Blue Willow Toastrite toaster should be valued around $4,000 for insurance replacement purposes—if it is in perfect condition.

Related item

Two-slot ceramic toaster with an on/off switch on the left, a two-prong plug receptor on the right, and a browning gauge on the front. The on/off switch is missing its decorative ceramic knob, which had a "bull's-eye" motif in the center. The piece has two handles and a textured surface that resembles a basket. It is decorated with representations of flowers. It has its original cord and is in working condition.

What is it?

There is some disagreement about when this particular toaster was made. Some sources say it was manufactured as early as 1928, others report a circa date of 1934, and still others just say "late 1930s."

Whatever the exact date may be (and we feel the 1934 date is probably the correct one), this ceramic pop-up toaster was made by the Porcelier Manufacturing Company of South Greensburg, Pennsylvania. The company was actually founded in 1927 in East Liverpool, Ohio, but in 1930, it moved to South Greensburg. It went out of business in 1954, but over its years of operation, it made items using "vitrified" or "vitreous" china that is not technically "porcelain" but is close.

Porcelier made a variety of items but specialized in such things as teapots, electric coffee pots, cream and sugar bowl sets, cups, bowls, and similar items. It made a very limited number of electric toasters, which came in several designs, all of which are somewhat rare and hard to find.

The one shown here is style or catalog number 5002. It is decorated with a transfer print that was created by Emil Hasentab, who was a company designer working in the 1930s (we suspect this eliminates the 1928 date mentioned previously). In any event, the pieces with the basket-weave design shown here were probably the most popular of Porcelier's designs, and this style can be found on coffee urns and coffee pots as well as on cream pitchers and sugar bowls.

When the toaster was added to this ensemble, the hostesses of the 1930s and '40s could entertain guests for breakfast in the dining room with a suite of elegant appliances. It was all very *Ozzie and Harriet*, and it was the sort of equipment that was necessary to achieve a style of ensuite entertainment that many American upscale homemakers wanted at the time.

As was said earlier, no Porcelier toaster is easy to find. The 5002, however, with its raised basket-weave design molded into the ceramic surface, is perhaps the most abundant of the examples made by this company.

What is it worth?

The missing knob on the on/off switch has very little impact on the value because these units are so hard to find, and the Porcelier 5002 shown here has an insurance replacement value of $1,750. A complete unit in perfect condition might be just a bit more.

Item 19

Westinghouse "Turnover Toaster"

Valued at $100

Electric toaster marked on the bottom "Turnover Toaster No. 284032A Westinghouse E&M Co. Mansfield, Ohio." The toaster is 7 inches tall and has a chrome-plated body with fiber feet and Bakelite knob handles. There is an on/off switch on the original cord, which is still in good condition. On the top, there is a metal plate with elongated cutouts in a sunburst style. The toaster is in good working order, and there is no pitting or discoloration on the metal.

What is it?

We have already discussed George Westinghouse at some length in the section on fans. The Westinghouse Company went into the appliance-making business in 1917, when it acquired the Copeman Electric Stove Company, which had been making stoves since 1914.

It moved the operation to Mansfield, Ohio, where this particular toaster was produced. The Westinghouse Electric and Manufacturing Company is said to have invented the "turnover" toaster, which made it possible to turn the toast over without touching it and burning your fingers. However, some toasters of this type indicate that the technology was based on patents from Copeman Electric Stove.

These toasters are generally said to have originated circa 1917, but some Westinghouse Turnover toasters can be found with an East Pittsburgh, Pennsylvania, address on the bottom, which is where the company was located before it moved to Mansfield. In any event, the Turnover toaster pictured here is also called a "wheel top" because of the platform attached to the top of the appliance.

The flat area could be used for several purposes. It could hold the toast after it was made to keep it warm, or it was large enough to hold a coffee pot to keep the liquid warm without having to return it to the stove. This particular example is circa 1920 and has the typical heating element of the day that consists of wire wrapped around a mica core.

What is it worth?

This is a very attractive toaster, but a large number of them were made, and they are still fairly available on the current market. This one, in excellent condition, is valued for insurance replacement purposes at $100.

Item 20
Elekthermax Toaster

Valued at $250
Electric toaster, 6¾ by 8½ by 4½
inches. Chrome-plated metal body
with black plastic knobs for handles
and a black plastic base.

What is it?

As a general rule, we have discussed mainly American objects in this book, but this toaster will be an exception because it is a really great looking toaster from Europe that can be found in several museums around the United States.

Well then, if this interesting-looking turnover toaster is not American, could it be French? No. Could it be English, German, or Italian? No. It is not a product of any of these countries, which have exported so many items to the United States over the years.

Instead, this toaster was made in Budapest, Hungary, in the 1930s by a company named Elekthermax, which is still in business today. This company began in Budapest in 1920 as Magyar Electhermas Reszvenytarsasaga. Currently, it is located in the town of Papa, Hungary, and makes large kitchen appliances and heating systems.

Earlier, we called this piece a turnover toaster, which means that it is designed to flip the bread over when the door opened so that both sides could be evenly browned. The body is stylishly made from chromed metal with two handles that have round black Bakelite knobs and a stepped Bakelite base in a form that is generally called *jugendstil*.

Jugendstil translates as "youth style," and this name was first used in 1896 in the influential weekly *Die Jugend*. The style is primarily associated with items from German-speaking countries, plus Scandinavia (where it is called the "National Romantic Style"), and some Central European countries, particularly Hungary because it was once part of the Austro-Hungarian Empire.

This style was widely used in architecture and the decorative arts. Even though often associated with the more familiar Art Nouveau movement, *jugendstil* is noted for its precise and hard edges, which are somewhat different from the naturalistic forms of Art Nouveau. This particular toaster is Elekthermax's VP-3 model, and even though this item was made somewhat later than most classical *jugendstil* pieces, the design of the base fits within this style. It should also be noted that Elekthermax made another toaster called the KP-5, which has shorter handles.

What is it worth?

The insurance replacement value for this Hungarian turnover toaster is $225.

Item 21
General Electric Toaster

Valued at $125

Electric toaster, 7½ inches tall and 11½ inches wide. The body is chrome with swirled brown Bakelite handles and a Bakelite band around the bottom. It is decorated with an impressed design of crossed stylized leaves bisected by an arrow accented with stars. The piece, which is marked "General Electric" and "cat, No. 159T77," has its original cloth-covered cord and is in working condition.

What is it?

Bread made with yeast probably originated in Egypt some 6,000 years ago, and the idea of toasting bread has been around for a very long time. Early on, the Romans and other cultures toasted bread as a way to preserve it. The word for "toast" is actually derived from the Latin word for to scorch or burn, which is ironic because the idea behind toast is not to scorch or burn it.

To make toast, bread is heated using a radiant heat source to 310 degrees Fahrenheit. At this point, a chemical change called the Maillard reaction takes place and the starches and sugars in the bread begin to caramelize and the bread itself takes on a new texture with more intense flavor. Get the bread too hot for too long and the grain fibers begin to turn into carbon—and that means burned toast.

Over the years, a number of different instruments have been used to get the bread hot and crusty without burning fingers. Some of our ancestors used the hearthstone to toast bread, others used a toasting fork to hold the bread over the flames, and some used wrought iron hinged bread holders that could be attached to the walls of the fireplace to swing in over the fire.

When electricity began flowing into our homes, many inventors wanted to create a device that would use this form of energy to toast bread, but there was a problem, and it was the same problem inventors had with the incandescent light bulb. To make a toaster (or an incandescent light bulb) work, a filament was needed that could be heated over and over again to red-hot temperatures without "burning out" or becoming brittle and breaking.

Perhaps the earliest toaster ever made was the "Eclipse," made by England's Compton and Company. This piece using iron wires for its heating element had a tendency to rust, melt, and start fires. It was, as one might imagine, not a success.

In 1905, Albert March patented an alloy of nickel and chromium that became known as "Nichrome." It had low electrical conductivity and was largely nonoxidizing, tough, ductile enough to be made into wires, and electrically resistant. In other words, when a current was run through this alloy, it would heat up rapidly and would not easily burn out.

Two months after the March patent, George Schneider of the American Electric Heater Company in Detroit applied for a patent on a toaster using such a wire, but this toaster was not a commercial success. This had to wait for the D-12 toaster, which was invented in 1909 by Frank Shailor of General Electric. This machine had a ceramic base and a plug that could be put into a light socket. Although General Electric's D-12 toaster is generally credited with being the first successful appliance of this nature, new evidence now suggests that Pacific Electric and Simplex made toasters that were as early or earlier.

Right after the end of World War I, Charles Strite, a mechanic in a plant in Stillwater, Minnesota, was getting tired of the company's cafeteria burning his toast all of the time. He fiddled around with some parts, such as timers and springs, and eventually invented the first pop-up toaster, which was patented May 29, 1919. These devices were available to restaurants in the early 1920s, but the first home model, the "Toastmaster," did not come out until 1926.

The pop-up toaster pictured here is in a typical streamline design that was popular during the 1940s. This particular piece was first made by General Electric in 1945 in its Bridgeport, Connecticut, and Ontario, California, factories. It has a delightfully modern look with a bright finish that was popular after the dark days of World War II.

What is it worth? Collectors are especially interested in the Bakelite detailing and the streamline design of this circa-1945 toaster. Its insurance replacement value is $125.

Item 22
"Twin-O-Matic" Waffle Maker

Valued at $250

Waffle maker, 5 by 11⅝ by 7¾ inches. Chrome finish with black plastic supports on a circular base. The top has incised lines with a gauge to allow the waffles to be baked from dark to light. The piece is marked with a label that reads "Twin-O-Matic Made by Manning-Bowman Company Meriden, Conn. U. S. America." The piece is in excellent condition with no pitting to the chrome body.

What is it?
When electricity started coming into homes, many homemakers began acquiring small appliances designed to save labor or produce a specialized product. Many times, these appliances were meant to be attractive and to be used to serve family and guests in the dining room.

One of these was the waffle maker, which could be used tableside or on the buffet. These waffle makers were often accompanied by attractive batter sets that could be brought from the kitchen holding the pre-prepared waffle makings ready to be poured in the new-fangled electric machine.

Waffles have been around for a very long time. They are made from a batter of a mixture of ingredients that typically includes flour, milk, eggs, butter, oil, and some kind of leavening. Waffles are thought to have originated in Europe during the late Middle Ages and were cooked in hinged, two part, plate-like waffle irons. The batter was poured into the bottom half of this device, the top was lowered, and the apparatus was placed into a fire to bake.

Waffles are two sided with a grid-like pattern on their surface that, in modern times, has generally been diamond or square shapes with crisscrossing ridges and deep valleys between. It is said that in the United States, the first waffles were made in 1620 by the Pilgrims, who brought the recipe from Holland.

The electric waffle maker shown here was made by the Manning-Bowman Company of Meriden, Connecticut. Some sources trace the company's roots back to Cromwell, Connecticut, where it was incorporated as a maker of Britannia (a type of metal similar to pewter) and tin wares in 1864. Another source, however, says that the company was founded in 1857 but not incorporated until 1887.

Most sources agree that financial difficulties forced Manning-Bowman to move to Meriden in 1872 under the control of the Meriden Britannia Company, and in 1898, the International Silver Company owned a majority of the stock. At that time, its major business was making silver-plated items, adding metal mountings to graniteware vessels, and making items from other kinds of metal such as nickel. In the early twentieth century, the company evolved into one of the major makers of small electrical appliances in the United States.

The very stylish Manning-Bowman waffle iron shown here is called the "Twin-O-Matic" and was designed by Karl Ratcliff to be displayed at the 1939 New York World's Fair. It was based on an idea of Charles Cole, who in 1926 came up with the notion for a waffle maker that made two waffles at once.

The concept behind this two-sided/two-waffle device was twofold. First, it allowed couples to make two waffles at once so that a husband and wife could each enjoy a hot waffle at the same time, and second, it saved on the electricity needed to make two waffles separately. This was important because in the 1920s and '30s, electricity could be very expensive at about 25 cents a kilowatt hour, which would be almost $8 a kilowatt hour in today's money.

When using the Twin-O-Matic, consumers were instructed to fill the top section with batter (the top section is the one with the raised bake-indicator in the center of the cover), wait fifteen seconds for the first waffle to set, and then flip the body over and pour in more batter. This procedure was then supposed to produce two perfect 8-inch diameter waffles almost simultaneously. It should be noted that other twin waffle makers made smaller waffles that were in the 4- to 6-inch diameter range.

The Twin-O-Matic won awards and has been featured in at least one book on Art Deco design even though it came along a bit late to qualify as true Art Deco. There are several interesting features on this particular waffle maker—one is the black or brown plastic supports, and another is the raised thermometer/thermostat in the top of one side of the waffle maker cover.

The rather dramatic plastic support is called a "trunion mount," and it is made from Bakelite. Bakelite is a trade name for the thermosetting phenol formaldehyde resin polyoxybenzylmethylenglycolanhydride. Since no one except a chemist could possibly remember or pronounce that name without doing damage to his or her teeth and tongue, another name was chosen for the public.

Bakelite was developed between 1907 and 1909 by Dr. Leo Baekeland, and it was the first plastic made from synthetic polymers. It was a perfect material for the modern age in that it was nonconductive for electricity and heat resistant. It was widely used in radios, telephones, early electric guitars, and small appliances because of these properties.

Another Twin-O-Matic feature that merits discussion is the raised "bake indicator" in the center of the cover. This is both a thermometer and a thermostat used to regulate the heating of the waffle iron so that it does not exceed the set temperature and over-cook or burn the waffle.

This is significant because Manning-Bowman made two very similar waffle makers. The Twin-O-Matic, which we have been discussing, had the raised thermometer/thermostat on the top cover, but the similar "Twinover" had only a thermometer that is set flush into the top cover. The Twinover is earlier than the Twin-O-Matic and is somewhat rarer. It is also considered to be worth more money than the Twin-O-Matic discussed here.

What is it worth? The circa-1940 Manning-Bowman Twin-O-Matic waffle maker should be valued at $250.

Item 23
Coffee Urn

Valued at $85

Chrome coffee urn with drop handles in brown swirled plastic, 15 inches tall. The piece has wooden ball feet and is decorated with three bands around the body that resemble the indentions made by hand hammering. The top has a glass knob marked "McKee" and "Glassbake U.S.A." The urn is in working order with all its original parts.

What is it? Starting right after the end of World War I, coffee brewers such as this one became very popular. This circa-1920 urn has a shiny chrome finish and Bakelite drop handles and spigot handle, and despite its thoroughly modern detailing, still pays homage to the American Arts and Crafts movement, which at the time this piece was made was gasping its last breath. This is seen primarily in the three bands around the body of the pot, which suggest hand-hammered construction but are actually just a pressed-in decoration.

The ready availability of household electricity meant that coffee no longer had to be brewed on the stove in the kitchen and transferred to a more attractive server to be brought to the table. Now, hostesses could put an attractive coffee urn on their buffets, brew it electrically, and then serve the hot beverage to guests.

Sometimes, coffee urns such as this one were made in sets that included a tray and a matching cream pitcher and sugar bowl. These sets are more desirable to collectors than the coffee urns alone, but attractive single pieces such as the example shown here are also of interest.

There is no manufacturer's name on this particular coffee urn, perhaps because the underside of the base has been cleaned so assiduously that the markings that once may have been there have now faded. However, it is also possible that this pot was never marked by the maker, as was sometimes the case with high-quality urns of this nature.

Many companies made coffee urns similar to this one, including Landers, Frary & Clark (under the trade name "Universal"), S.W. Farber Inc. (known for its "Farberware" line), Manning-Bowman, and the Continental Silver Company. From the shape of the lid and the wooden ball feet to the color of the Bakelite used on the drop handles, the urn shown here is reminiscent of items made by the Continental Silver Company of New York City. This firm was founded around 1920 and remained in business until about 1950.

The marks on the glass knob on this urn tell us for certain that it was made by the McKee Glass Company, which was founded in Pittsburgh, Pennsylvania, around 1834. Early on, this company made products such as bottles, fruit jars, window glass, telegraph line insulators, and pressed glass table wares. The company moved to Jeanette, Pennsylvania, in 1888 and remained in business until 1951.

What is it worth? Other than the over-cleaned bottom of the base, this coffee urn is in excellent working condition and has an insurance replacement value of $85.

Item 24

"Kitchen Aid" Coffee Mill

Valued at $100

Coffee mill with a white enameled base and a large glass jar, 13¾ inches tall. The base has a rectilinear spout with a cover with the words "Kitchen Aid" above. At the base in a triangular notch is "Model A-9 Coffee Mill The Hobart Mfg. Co. Troy, Ohio." The piece is in working order. The white enamel is in good condition.

What is it?

The company that made this home coffee grinder was founded July 20, 1897, as the Hobart Electric Manufacturing Company. In the early twentieth century, Hobart-manufactured motors were sold to merchants, who attached them (with the help of Hobart representatives) by means of a belt to the flywheels of previously hand-operated coffee mills, creating the world's first self-contained powered coffee mill.

Over the years, Hobart introduced such items as an electric meat chopper and a peanut-butter-making machine. Then in 1908, Herbert Johnson, an engineer for Hobart, invented the first commercial stand mixer after watching a baker mixing bread dough with a metal spoon.

This got him to experiment with making a mechanical counterpart, and by 1915, the Kitchen Aid Food Preparer—or stand mixer—was standard equipment in many of America's bakeries. After World War I ended, Hobart executives were taking experimental home mixers into their kitchens, and one of the wives said, "I don't care what you call it, all I know is that it is the best kitchen aid I've ever had." Legend says that the name "Kitchen Aid" came from this offhand remark.

These first Kitchen Aid mixers weighed in at about 65 pounds. In addition, they were not cheap. They had an initial cost of $189.50—more than $2,000 in today's dollars. These factors opened the door for Sunbeam to introduce its lighter, cheaper ($18.25) stand mixers in 1929.

Hobart and its Kitchen Aid brand are still very much leaders in the making of quality mixers and other small household appliances. The model A-9 coffee grinder shown here was introduced in 1937, and indications are that recent models are available. This particular one was probably made no later than the 1940s. It has a typical pot metal body, but is missing its original cleaning brush.

What is it worth?

This example is in good working order and has an insurance replacement value of $100.

Item 25
Dormeyer Mixer

Valued at $125
Electric mixer with twin beaters, a chrome body, and wooden handles, approximately 12⅞ by 5 by 4⅞ inches. It is marked "Dormeyer Corporation, Chicago Illinois, Pat. 1921 Other Pats Pending."

What is it?

A mixer is an almost indispensable tool in the modern kitchen. What present-day cook wants to hand mix a cake or beat egg whites until they form a perfect meringue?

The first patent for a mixer was taken out in 1885 by Rufus W. Eastman, whose revolutionary machine used electricity or water power. Despite this early development, mixers did not start coming into our homes in significant numbers until the late 1920s and early '30s.

Many companies made these pieces, and one of them was the A.F. Dormeyer Corporation of Chicago, Illinois, which evolved from the MacLeod Corporation. In the 1920s, Dormeyer introduced a hand-held electric mixer (or beater) with a Hamilton Beach motor.

It had a box-like motor housing above twin beaters that were held in a beater assembly with a squared-off base that allowed the unit to be freestanding in a bowl. Many collectors call this kind of device a "cake mixer." The example shown on the previous page has a vent in the case that resembles a sort of sunrise. Later models had vents that resembled the petals of a daisy arranged around the center.

The example pictured here, circa 1930, is in operating condition.

What is it worth?

The insurance replacement value is $125.

Item 26
Sunbeam "Mixmaster"

Valued at $45

Turquoise-colored electric mixer with glass bowl, 12 inches long by 13 inches tall. The mixer is marked "Sunbeam Mixmaster" on the side, and the glass bowl is marked "Glassbake 20CJ for Sunbeam." The rear end of the mixer has a large adjustable dial to allow the user to select from twelve speeds. There is damage to the enamel finish and some rust, but the piece is in working order.

What is it? There was a time when the name Sunbeam was synonymous with small appliances, especially electric mixers. Sunbeam traces its origins to the Chicago Flexible Shaft Company, which was founded in the early 1890s by John K. Stewart and Thomas J. Clark. This company made machinery for clipping and grooming horses.

By 1897, it was the leading maker of sheep-shearing equipment, and at the turn of the twentieth century, it was exporting large numbers of these apparatuses to the Cooper Sheep Shearing Machinery Proprietary in Australia. Between 1908 and 1936, Chicago Flexible Shaft Company was a subsidiary of the English company William Cooper & Nephews.

Around 1910, Chicago Flexible Shaft began making small appliances such as irons, toasters, waffle irons, coffee makers, and yes, electric mixers. Its first small appliance was the "Princess" electric iron. This was such a success that it paved the way for many other types of household gadgets.

In 1914, the company became Cooper Engineering, and the Sunbeam brand name did not emerge until 1921, when it was used in a national advertising campaign. Cooper Engineering changed its name to the Sunbeam Corporation in 1946 and chose the slogan, "Best Electric Appliances Made."

The first Sunbeam Mixmaster debuted in May 1929 and was model M4. As this model was updated, a letter code was added to the M4 designation—these are the M4A, M4B, M4C, M4F, M4H, and so on. These mixers were made from cast iron, had a 60-watt motor, and could not be removed from the stand to be used as a hand mixer. The speed control was on the base, and these units were very heavy.

The Mixmaster M4J was the first model to have a handle so that it could be used as a handheld unit, and the speed controls moved from the base to the rear of the motor housing. The Mixmaster Model 1 was Sunbeam's first ten-speed model, and there was a matching Mixmaster Jr.

This later device was conceived as a working "toy" that could be used by little girls to mix right along with mom. However, it was not particularly small—it had 25 watts of power, a 4-inch-diameter jadeite bowl (opaque green), and was approximately 9 inches tall.

The Mixmaster shown here is the Model 12, and is considered to be the last of the classic style Mixmasters. This Mixmaster has fins on its rear dial control, but it was not the first Mixmaster to have these. That honor goes to the Model 10, which was introduced in 1950 and had a Bakelite base and new front grill with parallel rows of slots.

The Model 11 (1955–1956) had round vents on the front grill, while the Model 12 has semicircular slots with a kind of semicircular projection over them. The Model 12 is said to be the first Sunbeam 12 speed mixer, but it actually ran the same speeds as the Model 11.

The Model 12 was manufactured between 1957 and 1967 and can be found in chrome, white, yellow, pink, and turquoise. Both pink and turquoise are eagerly sought after by collectors. The Model 12 was the best-selling Mixmaster ever made, and it is thought that significantly more than 4 million of these machines were sold during their ten-year existence.

What is it worth? In this condition, which is about average "as found," this Sunbeam Mixmaster electric mixer has an insurance replacement value of $45.

Item 27

"Juice-O-Mat"

What is it? People have been extracting juice from various kinds of citrus fruit since time immemorial. In the early twentieth century, however, juice reamers made from glass began to appear and became an integral part of modern kitchen equipment. These had a ridged cone shaped protrusion in the center of a shallow glass dish and often a handle on the side.

They were touted as devices that would bring health into the home, and mothers were urged to make fresh juice for their families. Using one of the glass reamers could be hard work and required a lot of "elbow grease" to produce a relatively small amount of juice.

In the modern age, an easier way to perform this tedious job was not long in coming. The resulting machine was the mechanical reamer or juicer in which the citrus fruit to be juiced was cut in half and placed in the jaws of the machine. A lever was then lowered to squeeze the juice from the fruit into the container that customarily came with the device.

Many companies made these items, but the one shown on page 99 is the Rival "Juice-O-Mat," which was invented by Joseph Ma-

Valued at $15

Mechanical juicer marked on the bottom "Single-Action Juice-O-Mat," approximately 8 inches tall, 7 inches deep, and 6 inches wide. The piece is made of steel covered with white enamel that has become very worn through constant use. It is missing its original collection cup.

jewski. The Rival Manufacturing Company was founded in Kansas City, Missouri, in 1932. Its Juice-O-Mat, which first appeared in that same year, was the first in their "O-Mat" or "O-Matic" line of small household appliances that were designed to "lighten the work load in the American home."

Other items in this line are the "Ice-O-Mat" ice crusher and the "Can-O-Mat" can opener (Rival produced the first electric can opener in 1945). The Juice-O-Mat can be found in several different configurations, and the one featured here is probably circa 1940.

Metal mechanical reamers such as this one are readily available on the current collectibles market, and because examples in really good condition are not all that hard to find, collectors severely downgrade those examples that are in less than perfect condition. Collectors are also more interested in colorful pieces other than white. We have seen Juice-O-Mats in shades of red, melon green, and yellow. Other colors probably exist.

What is it worth? Rival Juice-O-Mats in near perfect condition complete with their original juice cup bring prices in the $40 to $60 range, depending on their color. This example should be valued at $15.

Electric juicer with an enameled metal base, a separate milk glass bowl with spout, an aluminum perforated insert, and a porcelain reamer cone, 8 3/4 inches tall; the diameter of the milk glass bowl is 5 1/2 inches. The top is impressed "Handyhot Cat. No. 2700 Chicago Electric Mfg. Company," and on the side is a seal that reads "Sunkist Juiceit A Handyhot Product." It is operated with a toggle switch and rests on three rubber feet.

What is it?

In 1493, Columbus brought orange and lemon seeds to the New World, but it was not until 1769 that Father Junipero Sierra and his Spanish friars planted them in California. In 1804, the first large citrus grove was planted at Mission San Gabriel, and from there, citrus grew to be a major crop in Southern California.

Sunkist Growers Inc. does not grow oranges, but its members do—and they grow lots of them. This Arizona and California citrus growers membership cooperative has approximately 6,000 members and was formed in 1893 as the Southern California Fruit Exchange.

Around 1916, Sunkist started promoting a "Drink an Orange" advertising strategy to encourage more consumption of their growers' products. The idea was that if you ate an orange, you might eat just one, but if you turned it into juice for your family, the consumption would rise dramatically.

To promote the health benefits of citrus juice further, Sunkist had transparent green glass reamers made that had "Sunkist Oranges and Lemons" and "California Fruit Growers Exchange, Los Angeles" embossed on the side. In the 1920s, Sunkist advertisements in such magazines as *Good Housekeeping* included a coupon that would allow readers to write in and buy a Sunkist juicer for 50 cents. In the mid-1920s, Sunkist had the McKee Glass Company of Jeanette, Pennsylvania, produce Sunkist reamers in a rainbow of colors that included milk glass, transparent green, pink, custard, yellow, clear colorless, opaque pink, ivory, black, and teal blue, among several others (black is especially rare and valuable).

Glass hand-powered reamers are fine, but this was the modern age, and Sunkist also had its name put on an electric reamer called the Sunkist Juiceit that is pictured here. It was patented in 1934 and was made by the Chicago Electric Manufacturing Company using their trade name, Handyhot.

This company made a profusion of small household appliances including a toaster, a waffle iron, an ice cream freezer, a heater, a corn popper, and an automatic freezer defroster. It also produced a deluxe Juiceit model and another Sunkist Juiceit that had a roughly rectangular label on the front as opposed to the round label seen here.

This particular example is circa 1940.

What is it worth?
For insurance replacement purposes, this Sunkist Juiceit is worth $95.

Item 28
"Petipoint" Iron

Valued at $375
Electric iron made from chromium plated steel, steel, and Bakelite plastic, approximately 4½ by 10 by 5 inches.

What is it? Asking what this piece is may be a bit absurd because almost anyone who has ever worn clothes knows what an electric iron looks like. But this is a very special iron that has been called an "Electric Space Ship." This name is derived from the streamline fins that jut out from the side and look a bit like wings.

Prior to the 1930s, most irons were very heavy. Early examples were made from iron and were heated on a stove—and this made ironing during the summertime a form of torture that should have been outlawed by the Geneva Convention.

In any event, the first steam iron was called the Steam-O-Matic and was designed by Clifford Brooks Stevens. It was based on the principle that a steam iron did not have to be heavy to press out the wrinkles in fabric—a blast of steam would do that practically all by itself with very little pressure from the weight of the iron or the exertion of the human arm. This revolutionary iron made its initial appearance in 1938 and was first sold at Macy's in New York City. Clifford Brooks Stevens was born in Milwaukee, Wisconsin, in 1911, and at age 8, he came down with a severe case of polio. His limbs

stiffened, his right hand became virtually useless, and the doctors predicted that he would never walk again. Stevens' father thought differently.

He gave the bedridden boy a succession of models to build to increase his dexterity and provided sketchpads on which the lad could draw. He motivated his son to ride a bicycle and promised him a new car upon swimming a mile in a pool. Stevens is said to have tried hundreds of times to swim that mile until he succeeded and got his car.

In the 1930s, Stevens worked as an inventory manager for several companies, but he was bored and finally persuaded the management of one of the companies to allow him to redesign some product labels. In addition, he won a contract to revamp the logo for the company for which his father worked.

He opened his first industrial design office in 1935, and over the years, he and his staff were responsible for a number of remarkable designs such as the Miller Brewing Company logo, which is still in use today. The firm also contributed to the design of the

1949 Harley-Davidson Hydra-Glide motorcycle and the Willys Overland Jeepster.

In addition, Stevens and his associates were responsible for refining an idea that the Oscar Mayer Company came up with in 1936—namely the familiar and iconic Oscar Mayer Wienermobile. Originally, the Wienermobile was just a giant hot dog mounted on the bed of a truck, but in 1958, Stevens put the hot dog together with a bun to make the Oscar Mayer Wienermobile as we know it today.

Following the Steam-O-Matic iron mentioned on page 102, in 1941 (some sources say 1940), Stevens designed the "Petipoint" iron pictured on the previous page. It was designed for Milwaukee's Edmilton Company but manufactured by Waverly Tool of Sandusky, Ohio.

Many collectors consider this to be the ultimate in mid-century streamline irons, and it is eagerly sought after by collectors. There is a myth that this iron was first announced on Orson Welles' radio program as part of his Martian Invasion show that caused such a widespread panic. However, this is not possible because this broadcast took place October 30, 1938, some years before this piece was actually created.

What is it worth? This example of the model 410 Petipoint iron is in excellent condition and has an insurance replacement value of $375.

Related item

Electric iron, chrome-plated steel with black phenolic handle with a center section in clear red Lucite, 9 1/4 inches long. There is a square gauge under the handle with a clear cover that reads "American Beauty" and the settings "Linen," "Rayon," "Silk," and "Cotton." Above this is a round dial that is a heat gauge going from "Lowest Heat" to "Highest Heat." On top of this is an adjustment device shaped like a hemisphere with a long triangular lever piercing the center. Under the heel of the iron is "American Beauty," "Cat. No. 79AB," and "American Electrical Heater Company." The piece has its original cloth-covered cord.

What is it?

The American Electrical Heater Company was founded in Detroit, Michigan, in 1894. It primarily manufactured irons for clothes and soldering until it went out of business in the early 1990s.

Collectors are perhaps most familiar with American Electrical Heater's American Beauty line of irons that originated before World War I. These early models were fairly "plain Jane" from a design point of view, but the advertising promoted them as a device to "Make Ironing Day Easier—for both the June Bride and Every other Woman."

The model shown here was patented in June 1940 by F. Kuhn, et al., but it was not manufactured until after the end of World War II. It is reported that the first of these irons with the ruby Lucite insert in the center of the handle was initially manufactured in 1947 and is Model 79AB.

Lucite, a type of clear plastic, was discovered by DuPont in 1931. It is a methyl methacrylate plastic that is so clear and strong that it could be used for windshields and gunners' turrets during World War II. After the war, it was used to make everything from hairbrushes to lamps, tables, and even sculptures.

For this iron, the clear plastic has been tinted red and is flanked by sections of black phenolic resin plastic called Bakelite. This iron also came with an orange Lucite center in the handle (some sources call the color "amber"), and this is much rarer than the ruby examples, which are available in today's collectors market.

The examples with the amber or orange Lucite in the handle are Model number 33AB and were initially produced in 1951. These irons are good examples of American streamline design and have been featured in museum shows such as the Baltimore Museum of Art's "Masterpieces of American Design."

What is it worth?

This ruby-Lucite-handled American Beauty iron should be valued for insurance replacement purposes at $50 and is a good example illustrating that not everything found in a museum is hugely valuable.

Radios

Item 29
"Breadboard" Radio

What is it? The unit pictured here is known to collectors as a "breadboard" radio. These are sets from the early days of radio (the 1920s) and are characterized by the fact that the radio components are mounted on a rectangular board that usually has "breadboard ends." This phrase refers to narrow strips of wood that are attached at either end of the long base to strengthen and prevent splitting. The wood grain in the narrow strips runs perpendicular to the grain in the rest of the board.

Breadboard units do not have cases or cabinets, and all of the works are open to view. These ran on batteries and had no integral speaker. To hear a broadcast, listeners had to use headphones or purchase a separate speaker.

Arthur Atwater Kent was born in Vermont in 1873. His inventions are mainly associated with the automobile; he created the closely timed ignition system and a distributor that allowed for the use of a single coil.

The Atwater Kent Manufacturing Company of Philadelphia, Pennsylvania, began in 1896 as a manufacturer of parts and electrical items for use on automobiles. World War I and the recession that followed led the company to explore new business opportunities, and it decided to enter the new field of consumer radio. It began in

Valued at $1,100

Rectangular board-mounted radio with three dials with two tubes between them and a cluster of three tubes on the left, 29 inches long by 10 inches deep. The piece is marked "Atwater Kent" on a tag on the back.

1921 or 1922 by making component parts and introduced a large line of breadboard sets.

Atwater Kent produced its first sets with cabinets in 1924. It bought the required furniture from several manufacturers including the Pooley Corporation and the Red Lion Cabinet Company. For a time, Atwater Kent prospered. It became an important name in radio manufacturing, and from 1925 to 1927, it sponsored the popular "Atwater Kent Radio Hour." At one time, it was the largest radio factory in the world, but sadly, Atwater Kent never recovered from the Great Depression and went out of business in 1936.

The radio shown here is a Model 10C, which was introduced in 1924. This is a popular item, but of all the Atwater Kent breadboard models, the Model 5 is probably the most sought after. The Model 5 was introduced in 1923 and is much harder to find than the other Atwater Kent breadboard models. It was mounted on a small rectangular board with a left-side dial and five tubes on the right side. A Model 5 in excellent condition has an insurance value of about $4,500.

What is it worth? This Atwater Kent Model 10C is in good condition and has an insurance replacement value of $1,100.

Radio with oval medallion that has "Atwater Kent" in a rectangular reserve surrounded by a neoclassical wreath. There are three dials on the front, and the radio is in a wooden case with a black front that has a lift top. There are five tubes, and this model runs on batteries.

What is it?

This kind of radio is called a battery set, which is appropriate because like the breadboard sets before them, it ran on batteries. This power source was used because many—perhaps a majority—of American homes circa 1925 did not have household electricity.

Batteries were the prevalent power source, and homeowners generally took them to town once a week to have them recharged so that they would not miss their favorite programs during the upcoming week. Typically, radios required more than one battery for operation—one that was similar to an automobile battery to power the tube filaments and one or two additional batteries to provide power for other sections of the radio.

The early crystal sets amazed those who listened intently to the voices that came out of the air. But as the breadboard sets discussed earlier came into vogue, radios began to move into the living room, where they were often the center of household—and sometimes neighborhood—attention. Once they were in the "company" part of the house and the neighbors were coming over nightly to listen, homeowners started to want their radios to be more attractive—to look more like a piece of furniture.

In response to this consumer demand, companies began to enclose their sets in attractive boxes or cases that could sit on a table or look like a small piece of furniture. These units were still powered by batteries and still required a speaker to be purchased separately, but they did look better in the living room.

This particular example is the Atwater Kent Model 20, which is often referred to as the "Big Box," and was first made in 1925. There is a smaller version, the Model 20C, that is very similar and is called the "Compact" or "Small Box." Battery sets like this one were largely replaced by radios that ran on AC (alternating current) in the late 1920s, but it is reported that battery-operated radios similar to this one were made for use on farms right up until the late 1950s.

What is it worth?

Insurance replacement value of this Atwater Kent Model 20 Big Box is $200.

Item 30
Philco "Cathedral" Radio

Valued at $300

Table model radio with a rounded top, approximately 16 inches tall by 13 inches wide. There is a fabric oval on the front that is accentuated with cutouts and four tuning knobs, plus a roughly rectangular dial in the center. The cabinet itself is wood, and the word "Philco" is in gold on the center post. The piece is in good condition and still functions.

What is it?

Philco traces its origins back to 1892 and the Spencer Company, which was named after one of its founders, Thomas Spencer. The name was quickly changed to the "Helios Electric Company," and it initially made carbon arc lamps.

Located in Philadelphia, Helios struggled until it went into the battery business in 1906 and changed its name to the "Philadelphia Storage Battery Company." It did acceptable business with batteries for automobiles and trucks. But when the radio craze hit America in the early 1920s, it began making radio batteries in a big way.

It also manufactured something called a "Socket Power" unit or "battery eliminator," which allowed households wired with electricity to use radios that were designed and manufactured to be powered by batteries. This became a very big-selling product for Philco.

In 1927, the first AC (alternating current) radio tubes appeared, and it was evident that the era of battery-powered radios was at an end. Strategically, Philco switched to making radios and had its first huge seller with the Model 20 radio, which collectors call a cathedral radio.

The term cathedral radio refers to a specific type of table-model radio cabinet with a rounded or pointed top that resembles the profile of windows that are often seen in churches. When many people think "old radio," this is the image that comes to mind. It should also be mentioned that cathedral-model radios were often relatively inexpensive and therefore were affordable for many, if not most, American households.

Philco's Model 20 cathedral radio came out in 1930. The cathedral set seen here is a Model 60B, which was first sold in June 1934 and remained in production until 1936. The original selling price was $29.95, and it is one of four units to house Philco's Model 60 chassis. This is a five-tube receiver that could pick up standard broadcast signals as well as police, aircraft, airport, and amateur radiophone signals.

What is it worth?

This Philco Model 60B cathedral radio is in good condition and has an insurance replacement value of $300.

Item 31

Zenith "Waltons" Radio

Valued at $1,800

Table-model radio in an essentially rectangular wooden cabinet with a slightly arched top. The top third of the cabinet has a fabric-covered speaker that is separated by three bars of wood that go over the top of the case. The large "airplane dial" in the center of the lower half of the case is contained within a triangular form with curved sides. At each point of the triangle there is a knob. The word "Zenith" appears on the dial.

What is it?

Zenith had rather humble beginnings in Chicago, Illinois, in 1918 as the Chicago Laboratories. Its first "factory" was a kitchen table where two wireless enthusiasts assembled radio equipment for other amateur radio aficionados. The name for the new enterprise was derived from the radio call sign of the company's founder, Commander E. F. McDonald. His call sign was 9ZN, and in 1919, a new receiver, called the "Z-Nith," was installed at the radio station.

As the radio craze grew, so did the Zenith Radio Corporation, which was incorporated in 1923. In 1924, it introduced the first portable radio, and in 1926, it is said to have made the first radio that ran on ordinary household current. Zenith is credited with pioneering AM and FM broadcasting, and this includes the stereo FM broadcasting system that is still in use today. In 1927, it adopted its famous slogan: "The Quality Goes In Before The Name Goes On."

Zenith made all kinds of radios, including consoles, cathedrals, and a "tombstone" radio that has become famous and very desirable to collectors because it appeared as a prop on an extremely popular television show, *The Waltons*, on the air from 1972 to 1981. This homey show is still popular, and the Zenith radio that was shown in the Walton home has become something of an icon because it was associated with the doings on Waltons Mountain. Ironically, in the television show, this radio was supposed to belong to a struggling family with many children. But in real life, this set was one of Zenith's more expensive models.

A tombstone radio is a table model that gets its name because of its shape—tall and rectangular, with a flat, slightly curved or shaped top. These are also called "upright table models." This Zenith radio was introduced in 1938 and came in several models. There was the seven-tube model, which was 7-S-232 and originally cost $74.95; the nine-tube model, which was 9-S-232 and originally cost $89.95; and the twelve-tube model, which was 12-S-232 and originally sold for $99.95. The model shown here is the 9-S-232. Of the three, the 12-S-232 is the hardest to find.

There were differences among these three models besides the number of tubes they contained. The 7-S-232, for example, did not have the motorized tuning that the other models had. The 9-S-232 featured here had a 6T5 green tuning eye, which is a special vacuum tube that is mounted so that it is visible from the front of the set.

The 6T5 was used to aid the listener in tuning the radio by indicating the strength of the station. The display seems to open and close to indicate the strength of the signal. The name is derived from the fact that the device looks something like an "eye." These accessories are also called "cat's eye" or "magic eye" tuning.

The Zenith 9-S-232 tuned from 5 kilohertz (kilocycles) to 18.4 megacycles and had motorized electric tuning and a "robot dial." A robot dial is also called a shutter dial because there is a metal plate or shutter that determines the particular band being displayed. There are three separate dials on this Zenith robot dial, which select standard broadcast bands as well as shortwave, and police and amateur bands. Only one dial is visible at any one time, and the dial that is desired can be selected with a lever. Robot dials are typically associated with Zenith products, and they were first introduced on the 1938 models.

As a type of radio, most tombstone radios are not expensive on the current marketplace. But the Zenith 232 series of tombstones are hot because of their association with *The Waltons* and because they are rather hard to find.

What is it worth? The 9-S-232 Zenith "Waltons" radio shown here has an insurance replacement value of $1,800. The 7-S-232 is worth a bit less at $1,500. We could not find an exact price quoted for the scarce 12-S-232, but it exceeds $2,500.

Related item

Table model radio in wooden case, 22 inches tall and 16 inches at its widest. The piece has four knobs plus an oval dial and a speaker opening covered in cloth with cutouts. The case is a tall table model with slightly shaped shoulders and is in good condition.

What is it?
This radio is included to demonstrate that not all tombstone radios are as valuable as the Zenith "Waltons" model.

This is an attractive Philco Model 116B "tombstone" radio that was made circa 1936. It has six tubes and a lighted tuning meter-type dial. The shaped shoulders are a bit unusual for a tombstone radio of this type; but best of all, it picks up both regular broadcast channels as well as shortwave bands.

What is it worth?
The insurance replacement value is $200.

Item 32
Zenith Console Radio

Valued at $1,200

Console or floor model radio. The front is dominated by a large dial surrounded by a decorative escutcheon. The dial is marked with the Zenith logo and has such notations as "Weather Band," "Long Distance," "Foreign Broadcast," and "Standard Broadcast" among others. In addition, there are four tuning knobs below the large dial.

What is it? Console radios such as this one played an important role in the American home before the coming of television. A console radio is a floor model enclosed in a cabinet that may be on feet or legs or simply a tall rectangular box that is higher than it is wide and designed to rest on the floor. As we have said, the radio quickly evolved from the breadboard sets that were just tubes mounted on a rectangular board to the battery sets that were held in a low box-like cabinet to table models such as cathedral and tombstone sets. Finally, as radios became the center of family entertainment, the console radio became commonplace in many American homes.

The console was a full-fledged piece of furniture taking floor space like other pieces of living-room furniture. In some cases, it was not possible to tell that the fancy cabinet actually contained a radio until the doors were opened. At first glance, a console radio in one of these cabinets with fancy doors might just as easily have been a bar, a china cabinet, or even a desk.

Some of these sets were snazzy in the extreme and meant to occupy a proud place in an upscale living room, while others were just tall, rectangular, utilitarian radios that could be found in ordinary homes across the country and around the world. Zenith made a lot of floor-model radios, many of which were rather pricey when they were new.

The example shown here is the Zenith Model 12-A-57, and when it was first made in 1936, it retailed for $139.95, which was a significant amount of money at a time when the nation was still struggling with the privations of the Great Depression. This console set, however, is less costly than the 16-A-61, which was also introduced in 1936, and at first glance, appears to be similar in styling to the 12-A-57.

The 16-A-61 was part of Zenith's premier "Stratosphere" line. At the time, consumers might have thought these were so named because their prices, along with the music, seemed to come from the stratosphere. The 16-A-61 was the entry-level Stratosphere, and when it was new, it cost $375. Today, the 16-A-61 in good condition retails for more than $15,000, while the top of the line Stratosphere, the Model 1000-Z, retails above the $50,000 level (in good condition)!

The 12-A-57 is not nearly as exalted as these Stratosphere models, but it is a good console radio that has great styling. The large dial in the top center is called a Magnavision dial, which was a bold departure from the small, hard-to-read dials that were the norm. This multicolored dial was designed to help listeners distinguish between the different foreign shortwave bands and the domestic radio bands. This dial glowed in red, white, and green; and in the dark, it must have looked like something out of science fiction.

This set had "Split-Second" and "Shadowgraph" tuning that allowed access to six wave bands on four dial ranges. The term "Shadowgraph" refers to a tuning aid that was developed by Philco as the "Shadowmeter" in 1932. Zenith's version, the Shadowgraph, can be seen on this Zenith model as the small, roughly rectangular dial above the large Magnavision dial. It lit up brightly when the set was tuned to a strong signal and dimmed as the signal weakened.

In addition to the above, this Model 12-A -57 set had twelve tubes and an "Auditorium Dynamic" speaker. In 1936, this was not the top of the line, but it was a fine set that is still desired by today's collectors.

What is it worth? This Zenith Model 12-A-57 console radio has an insurance replacement value of $1,200 in this condition.

Item 33

Sparton "Bluebird" Radio

Valued at $3,500

Table model radio, 14¾ inches tall with 14½-inch-diameter round mirror. The piece is made from chrome and glass and has wooden ball feet. The center of the round dial reads "Sparton" over two globes with Jackson, Michigan, printed below. This dial has three chrome bars that run through it across the front of the radio. There are three knobs, and the mirror is blue with some losses to the backing and some speckling on the surface.

What is it?

William Sparks was born in Burrington, England, in 1882, and moved to Jackson, Michigan, when he was 9 years old. He graduated from Jackson High School and Delvin Business College and was determined to have a successful career in business.

In 1900, he joined with Phillip and Winthrop Withington to form the Sparks-Withington Company, which initially made parts for buggies. It was a very small company, but soon it became involved in the manufacturing of parts for those new-fangled automobiles. By 1929, Sparks-Withington had more than 7,000 employees.

In 1926, Sparks-Withington began to manufacture radios under the Sparton brand name. The first radios they made were fairly run-of-the-mill wooden table and console models. But in the early 1930s, a change occurred when famed designer Walter Dorwin Teague designed some modern-looking radios for the company.

Teague (1883–1960) was one of the pioneers of industrial design in the United States. His company, Walter Dorwin Teague Associates, is still an important industrial design consultation firm. Teague studied art at the Art Students League of New York (1903–1907), and he began his career creating graphic designs and illustrations for magazines.

People started asking Teague for his advice on product configuration, and in 1926, he opened an office specializing in industrial design. Over the years, he designed cameras for Eastman Kodak and is widely associated with the Kodak "Brownie" camera. He also contributed to the design of the Marmon automobile, Steuben glass, Texaco, and Boeing Aircraft (he designed the Boeing Stratocruiser's passenger compartment). Teague also created exhibits for the 1939 New York World's Fair.

For Sparks-Withington, he designed a line of radios that are characterized by their incorporation of blue or peach mirrors into the bodies of the radios. These are sometimes referred to as "Art Deco glass radios," and they are some of the most desired of all of the collectible radios.

They came in several models. One grouping is called the "Sled" and was Sparton's Models 557 and 558. These were rectangular with chrome horizontal fins that wrapped around one end, a square dial and feet that look a bit like sled runners. The Model 557 had three knobs, while the 558 had four. The Sled models were made circa 1936 and are valued at more than $2,000 depending on condition and color of the mirror. The peach mirrors are far rarer and are somewhat more valuable than the cobalt blue examples.

The Sparton mirrored radio pictured here is the Model 506 "Bluebird," which was made circa 1935. Like the other Sparton mirrored radios, this model was very expensive when it was new. Unfortunately, the mirrored surfaces on these radios were very susceptible to damage, and few have survived over the years in good condition.

The most valuable of all of the Sparton models is not a table model like the others but a floor model called "Nocturne." It is 46 inches tall and round like the Bluebird, but has parallel chrome lines running horizontally with vertical chrome running between them. This radio has two chrome feet, a "Frogeye" tuning indicator, and a large rectangular speaker below. This is said to be the most valuable of all American-made radios, and one in good condition is worth in excess of $40,000 on today's market.

What is it worth? These radios were prone to being broken or badly chipped, and the luster on the mirror often became speckled and/or rubbed off. The blue mirror finish on this example is worn in places, but it should be valued at $3,500.

Item 34
Majestic "Charlie McCarthy" Radio

Valued at $2,500

Table model radio with a plastic case, approximately 7½ inches wide by 6 inches tall by 7 inches deep. To one side of the case, there is a metal figure of a monocled gentleman attired in formal evening clothes with top hat and cane perched on a ledge. There are two knobs and a slide rule dial, and the radio is in good overall condition.

What is it?

The gentleman on this radio is "Charlie Mc-Carthy," a ventriloquist's dummy operated by the legendary Edgar Bergen and perhaps the most famous dummy of all time. Bergen made his alter ego into a sharp-tongued rascal, and after a sexy exchange on the air with Mae West in 1937, it is said that she was banned from radio for the next fifteen years.

Bergen was born in 1903 and taught himself the art of ventriloquism when he was a mere lad of 11. A few years later, he commissioned a carpenter named Theodore Mack to carve a block of pine into the likeness of a Chicago Irish newspaper boy by the name of "Charlie," and Charlie McCarthy was born.

In the beginning, Bergen and Charlie McCarthy worked in vaudeville and one-reel movies, but then Noel Coward recommended the duo for an appearance on a radio program hosted by crooner Rudy Valle. The public liked the duo so much that the next year they got their own radio show.

Bergen and Charlie McCarthy were on the air from 1937 to 1959. During that time, they were joined by the dimwitted "Mortimer Snerd" and man-crazy "Effie Klinker." Charlie McCarthy, however, was the undisputed star, and he was depicted as a debonair, girl-crazy child in adult clothes.

Bergen and Charlie McCarthy may have been inadvertently responsible for the hysteria surrounding Orson Welles' celebrated *War of the Worlds* radio play. It seems that millions of Americans listened to the popular ventriloquist act and missed the beginning of the Welles show, when it was made perfectly clear that it was a radio play. A little less than a quarter-hour into the Bergen show, the musical portion began. This was called *The Chase and Sanborn Hour*, and large numbers of listeners switched to the Welles show. There, they had the literal bejeebers scared out of them because they thought they were listening to a live newscast and not a piece of radio fiction.

Bergen and Charlie McCarthy made movies together, and in 1938, Bergen was given an honorary Oscar carved out of wood. Bergen and friend also did the television show *Do You Trust Your Wife?* starting in 1956. Bergen died in 1978 at age 75; Charlie McCarthy retired to the Smithsonian Institution in Washington, D.C., and has not spoken a word since.

The radio shown here, with its representation of a jaunty Charlie McCarthy on the front, was made by the Majestic Radio and Television Corporation of Chicago, Illinois, circa 1938. This is its Model 1 and it has six tubes and receives only ordinary broadcast bands.

Majestic traces its beginnings to the Grigsby-Grunow Company, which was a partnership between William Carl Grunow and Bertram James Grigsby, who reportedly manufactured automobile accessories in 1921. By 1924, they were making radio horn speakers, and in 1925, they were selling "A" and "B" radio battery eliminators with the trade name "Majestic."

In 1928, Grigsby-Grunow began making Majestic radios, which initially were very successful because the radio speakers were superior to those being made by other radio manufacturers. Unfortunately, the company was a casualty of the Great Depression, and in 1933, it went out of business only to reorganize as the Majestic Radio and Television Corporation.

Majestic Radio was one of the first companies to make radios powered by AC that did not rely on batteries. It began production of television sets before the beginning of World War II, but full-scale production did not begin until 1948. It ended in 1958. Over the years, Majestic made all kinds of radios, but the Model 1 Charlie McCarthy shown here is by far the most widely known and most eagerly sought after by collectors.

Beware: In many instances, the figure is missing its monocle, but in this case, the original is in place.

What is it worth? This Charlie McCarthy radio by the Majestic Radio and Television Corporation is valued at $2,500.

Item 35
Emerson "Snow White" Radio

Valued at $1,900

Small table-model radio depicting Snow White and the Seven Dwarfs, approximately 7½ by 7½ inches. The Snow White figure has a blue jewel on her dress, and there are acorn-shaped tuning knobs. The piece is in good overall condition with some rubbing to the paint.

What is it? It is believed by some that the iconic 1937 Disney motion picture *Snow White and the Seven Dwarfs* was the first full-length animated feature film, but it was not. That honor belongs to an Argentinean work titled *El Apostol*, but *Snow White and the Seven Dwarfs* was the first full-length animated feature to be filmed in Technicolor and the first to be a huge success throughout the English-speaking world.

The film was almost not made. Walt Disney's brother Roy was against it, as was Walt's wife, Lillian, and the Hollywood naysayers called it "Disney's Folly." Three years after the start of production and $1.5 million (a huge chunk of change in those days), the film premiered December 21, 1937, and was an immediate hit. Little girls everywhere wanted to be Snow White and eventually run off with "Prince Charming."

Disney's victory over all of the doubters came when the Academy Awards were passed out and he was awarded an honorary one for "a significant screen innovation which has charmed millions and pioneered a great new entertainment field." Shirley Temple presented the award, and the statuette was a full-sized Oscar surrounded by seven little Oscars.

The Emerson radio shown on page 128 dates from about 1939 and came in two versions. There was a large model that looks very similar to the one pictured here except the cottage continues on to the right with a doorway under a tree. The doorway has the tuning dial with two acorn-shaped knobs below. This smaller version lacks the tree and the doorway, and the turning dial was in the window with the acorn knobs among Snow White and the four dwarfs by her side.

The Emerson Radio and Phonograph Corporation was founded in 1922 by Benjamin Abrams and his brothers, Max and Louis. The Abrams boys had been born on a farm in Rumania, and Benjamin came to this country in 1905 when he was 12. Benjamin never attended high school and worked at a number of jobs including piano tuning, magazine sales, and finally phonograph and record sales.

Benjamin was joined in the United States by his brothers after a few years and eventually bought out (with borrowed money) the Emerson Record Company. In 1924, it produced its first radio-phonograph combination, and later it was the first company to produce a midget radio, a clock radio, a self-powered portable radio, a transistorized pocket radio, and a portable air conditioner. Emerson is famous for its Art Deco and streamline designed radios, and eventually, it also manufactured television sets, air conditioners, and tape recorders.

The cabinet on this radio is made from a product called "Repwood," which is composed of ground wood mixed with glue and then shaped in a mold. This material gives the appearance of carved wood and was often finished with colored lacquers or brown paint.

Some collectors report that Emerson sent the undecorated radios to Disney artists, who applied the paint to the front of the cabinet, but that is open to confirmation and conjecture. The model number on the radio pictured here is Q-236, while the large unit is model DB-247 and BM-247 (this latter unit has an airplane-style dial).

What is it worth? All of the Emerson *Snow White and the Seven Dwarf* radios are highly collectible. The large size DB-247 is valued for insurance replacement purposes at around $3,900 (depending on condition), while the Q-236 pictured here has an insurance replacement value of $1,900.

Item 36
Fada "Bullet" Radio

Valued at $1,200

Plastic radio, 10 inches wide by 6 inches tall. The body is burgundy plastic with a large round dial surrounded by a butterscotch yellow plastic with two matching knobs. There is also a plastic handle on top of the case in the butterscotch color. The large dial is marked "FADA."

What is it? The name "Fada" is derived from the first initials of the owner's name, Frank Angelo D'Andrea. He established his company in 1920, making crystal sets. Starting in 1923, he expanded his business to produce radios including battery sets, and still later, radios with wooden cabinets. Unfortunately, he experienced labor problems and eventually his company became a victim of the Great Depression. In 1932, the company was sold and the name was changed to Fada Radio and Electric Company. This company lasted until sometime in the late 1940s or perhaps as late as 1950.

Fada (even though the name appears in all capitals on radio dials, the correct form is capital "F" followed by lowercase "ada") is perhaps best known for the radios that it made from "Catalin," a type of plastic similar to Bakelite, but able to be produced in bright colors. The set seen on page 131 is the Model 1000 "Bullet," which is considered by many to be a prime example of 1940s streamline design. Its lines are sleek, and with its rounded end, it does indeed bear a striking resemblance to a bullet.

The Bullet cabinet seen on this radio was used on five different Fada models, the first of which was introduced in 1940. This was the Model 116, which received the standard broadcast bands plus shortwave. The Model 115 came out in 1941 (according to most sources), and received only the regular broadcast bands. These two Bullet radios each had five tubes.

The Fada Model 200 differed from the two models mentioned above by having six tubes, and the Model 189 is called the "All American" because it came in shades of red, white, and blue Catalin (this All American model is considered quite rare). The outbreak of World War II caused the production of radios for civilian use to be curtailed, and production of the final Bullet radio did not begin again until 1945 (some sources say 1946) with the Model 1000 shown here.

The Model 1000 was very popular with post-war consumers, and lots of these were sold. Therefore, the pre-war models of the Bullet are somewhat rarer than the post-war edition, but not necessarily more valuable. The Model 1000 did not have a set that offered shortwave like the pre-war Bullets, and they can be found with several tube configurations (some had six tubes, some reportedly had eight, and so forth).

There is one very interesting variation on the Model 1000 that needs to be mentioned. For most Model 1000s, the front grill is an integral part of the set and is in the same color plastic, but on some sets, there is an "inset" grill that was molded separately and set into the case. This was done because the grill was damaged when the case was taken out of the mold. To save the case, a new grill in a contrasting color of Catalin was inserted into the case so that it could be used.

Many collectors are very interested in Catalin plastic. Catalin is the trade name of the Catalin Corporation, which produced this type of phenol formaldehyde resin. In Spanish, the word means "pure," which may refer to the fact that Catalin does not have the fillers found in Bakelite.

As mentioned earlier, Catalin was similar to Bakelite except it could be produced in vivid colors, and some people actually refer to Catalin as "colored Bakelite." Catalin was also translucent, and along with the rainbow of colors, this is one of the main ways to distinguish Catalin from Bakelite quickly.

Catalin begins as a plastic that is uncolored and almost transparent. Before it is molded, liquid Catalin (Bakelite is formed from a powder) has a coal tar dye added to it to achieve the desired bright color. If a swirled effect with a contrasting color or shade is desired, the second color is introduced just before the Catalin is poured into the mold.

One of the main drawbacks to Catalin is that it is unstable, and the colors will darken over time. The Fada Model 1000 looks as if it has a beautiful butterscotch handle, knobs, and ring around the airplane dial, but when it was first made, these sections were actually white. Time has distinctively changed the hue, and many collectors try to restore their old Catalin radios by removing the oxidized layer. Repolishing a Catalin cabinet to uncover the original color can be a bit tricky, and we actually prefer the warm, mellow butterscotch to the white and think of the color change as a type of "patina."

An even more serious form of discoloration is called "tube burn" and occurs when the hot tubes inside the radio have caused the sections of the case located beside or above these tubes to darken considerably. This can be extremely unsightly, and collectors try to avoid cases with noticeable "tube burn."

Catalin also tends to shrink and this can cause radio cases to crack. When this happens, it constitutes a serious condition problem for most collectors. Catalin cases can shrink so much that the chassis cannot be removed, and this too is a major problem. Any significant cracking in a Catalin case can greatly reduce the monetary value of the radio. Luckily, the example shown here has only small and insignificant stress fractures around the places where chassis screws are attached.

Catalin cases were made for radios—such as this Fada Model 1000—for only a short time because of the problems mentioned, plus it was harder to work with and more expensive than other materials such as Bakelite. Making a Bakelite case, for example, took only a few seconds, while a Catalin case had to be cured for several days in a special oven and then hand finished. Catalin cases for radios were made only between about 1935 and 1947 because of all these problems.

What is it worth?
A Fada Bullet Model 1000 with unusual color combinations can bring several thousand dollars (radios in blue and green Catalin are the rarest and most valuable), but the burgundy/butterscotch color scheme seen here is fairly typical. The insurance replacement value for this table model set is $1,200. (Note: We found a maroon/alabaster Fada Bullet with an insert grill priced just a little less than $6,000 and a Model 115 Fada Bullet in blue for $2,750.)

Related item

Fada plastic radio, 9 inches wide by 6 1/2 inches high by 6 1/2 inches deep. It is burgundy and marked "FADA." This radio is primarily rectilinear with an arched top and flared base. There is a loop handle, a square dial on the right front side, and horizontal wrap-around louvers that are perpendicular to the dial. There are also two knobs.

What is it?
This radio is known as the "Bell" radio because it looks a little bit like a rather squat bell. It was introduced by Fada in 1939, and the set receives regular broadcast channels and shortwave. It has five tubes and is powered by AC/DC.

This radio came in a variety of Catalin colors including this burgundy, which at one time was probably a somewhat lighter shade. Two-toned models were also available such as blue/white, green/yellow, and yellow/red (the yellow was probably originally white).

This is a desirable Fada Catalin radio, and prices for rare colors have exceeded $7,000 at auction.

What is it worth?
The insurance replacement value for this Fada Bell in burgundy Catalin is $2,750.

Item 37
Garod "Commander" Radio

Valued at $2,500

Rectangular table-model radio with
plastic case in two contrasting colors—
red and alabaster, 11 inches wide by 6¾
inches tall by 6⅛ inches deep. There is a
slide-rule dial on the upper front of the
case, and below that are horizontal
wrap-around louvers. There is a handle
on top of the case and two knobs. At the
bottom is the name "Garod."

What is it?

In 1921, a company named Gardner-Rodman began making crystal radio sets in Brooklyn, New York. Two years later, it changed its name to the Garod Radio Corporation (a name derived from the initial letters in the names of the partners) and began manufacturing radios with tubes.

Unfortunately, Garod experienced some legal and quality-control problems that put it out of business in 1927. Most sources say the company was in and out of business until the name reappeared in 1933 as the Garod Corporation. In this incarnation, it made radios in Newark, New Jersey, and from 1947 to 1950, it manufactured television sets.

The radio shown here is known as the "Commander" and is Garod's Model "6AU-1." This model is very rectangular, and some critics say that this radio is an unimaginative design that is saved by the bright Catalin colors—but that evaluation may not be universally shared. True, the radio is rectangular and unashamedly so. The series of wrap-around louvers that make up most of the design emphasize this rectilinear nature and turn it into a virtue.

This radio pays tribute to what might be called the second branch of the Art Deco style. The first branch is the familiar style that is rather voluptuous with design elements depicting lush representations of fruit, flowers, and beautiful women in the "flapper" mode of the 1920s. The other branch is derived from industry and the machine and advocated straight, clean lines, squares, and rectangles. It also advocates the use of alternative "modern" materials such as chrome—and later—plastic. The Garod Commander meets all of these criteria and is certainly in the spirit of Art Deco even if it were made during the late 1940s after the Art Deco period had seen its heyday.

The Commander was made circa 1946 in a variety of Catalin colors, some in a single color and some two-toned. Alabaster (that has turned to various other shades through aging), red, and combinations of red and alabaster were made, but examples in blue and green are rare and very desirable.

The Garod Commander receives only ordinary broadcast channels, has six tubes, and runs on AC/DC power. Today, examples in good condition are hard to find because many exhibit cracking, chipping, and unsightly dark spots from "tube burn."

What is it worth?

The insurance replacement value for this red Catalin Garod Commander is $2,500. That price would be somewhat higher for models in rare shades such as green and blue.

Item 38
Coca-Cola Cooler Radio

Valued at $900

Radio shaped like a Coca-Cola cooler
with a red-and-white-painted plastic
body, 7 by 12 by 9½ inches. The front has
"Drink Coca-Cola" above with "Ice Cold"
below. There are two knobs between
these inscriptions and a black "slide
rule" dial above. There is a speaker grill
to one side. The radio is in excellent
playing condition, with some scratches
and other blemishes to the surface.

What is it?

There is no question that the soft drink Coca-Cola and the images that are associated with it are American icons that are known throughout the world. The first formula for Coca-Cola was reportedly concocted by "Doctor" (he was a pharmacist) John Smith Pemberton in a three-legged kettle in his backyard. The new product was reportedly named by Pemberton's accountant, Frank M. Robinson, and it is said that because of the fine penmanship he employed in his line of work, Robinson scrolled the logo that is now so familiar everywhere on the planet.

Coca-Cola was originally marketed as a "brain and nerve tonic," and the first sales were at Jacob's Pharmacy in Atlanta, Georgia, on May 8, 1886. Pemberton claimed that his drink cured various ailments such as morphine addiction, dyspepsia, headaches, and impotence. Yes, Coca-Cola was initially sold as being something like the "Viagra" of the day and contained 5 ounces of coca leaf (cocaine) for every gallon of syrup.

Initially, Coca-Cola was not very successful; and an average of only nine servings a day were made for the first eight months of sales—at just 5 cents per serving, nobody was getting rich very fast. Sales for the first year were just $50, and expenses for advertising came to $73.96.

There is a story that during summer 1886, a man with a headache came in and asked the "soda jerk" behind the soda fountain to mix up a bottle of Coca-Cola to cure his problem. Supposedly, the "soda jerk" was a lazy fellow and did not want to walk down to the end of the counter to get the regular tap water that was normally used to concoct the beverage. The "soda jerk" asked the customer if he could use carbonated water, which was conveniently at hand, instead. The customer liked the taste and fizz of the drink, and this is how Coca-Cola is said to have become carbonated.

In 1887, Pemberton sold a portion of his company to Asa Griggs Candler, who eventually took over the company. Like Pemberton, Candler was a pharmacist, but unlike Pemberton, he was a good businessman and promoter of his product. By the late 1890s, Coca-Cola had become America's most popular soda fountain drink.

Starting around 1894, Coca-Cola in bottles became available, but the bottles were not the ones that are so recognizable to consumers today. They were called "Hutchinson bottles," and they had straight sides with embossed printing that identified the name of the product and the location of the bottler. It was not until 1915 that the famous Coca-Cola bottle—called the "hobble skirt" or "Mae West"—began being used.

Advertising has always been a mainstay of Coca-Cola's success, and the variety of items bearing the company's logo is staggering. There are pocket mirrors, serving trays, lamps, tin plates, jewelry, pens and pencils, door push plates, bookmarks, school crossing signs, and a plethora of other things—including radios.

Today, the market is flooded with novelty radios that can be found in the shape of everything from a can of Spam and a carton of McDonald's french fries to the Statue of Liberty and a Budweiser can. These are all collectible, but most of these are modern transistor radios.

Over the years there have been several novelty Coca-Cola radios including ones shaped like vending machines that first appeared in the 1960s. There are, however, three vintage Coca-Cola radios that have tubes and are very desirable to today's collectors.

The first of these was made by Crosley Radio Corporation of Cincinnati, Ohio. It was introduced in 1933 and is in the shape of a 24-inch-tall bottle. These are seldom found with working radios, but collectors should be warned not to replace the original works with a radio that functions. In good, original condition, we have seen this radio valued for as much as $4,500, and replacing the innards causes it to lose considerable value.

The radio pictured here was made by Point-Of-Purchase Displays and is Model 5A410A. It was first made in 1949. The case is red painted plastic—often referred to as being "red painted Bakelite." The lettering is painted white, and the trim is silver. It is important that the case be in good shape, but replaced power cords are not a deduction.

There was a radio similar to this one except that it was a clock radio and had a large round dial below "Drink Coca-Cola." In good condition, the clock-radio version of the Coca-Cola cooler radio is valued at $1,400.

What is it worth? The insurance replacement value for a circa-1949 Coca-Cola cooler radio is $900.

Televisions

Item 39
Admiral Bakelite Television

Valued at $750

Floor model
television, 32 inches
tall by 17 inches
wide. Below the
screen in cursive is written
"Admiral" and below that are four
tuning dials. The speaker is covered
with a gold cloth and lattice work.
The entire case is made from
plastic. The set is in working order.

What is it? The Admiral Corporation was founded in Chicago, Illinois, in 1934 by Ross David Siragusa and four other investors. Siragusa sold almost everything he owned—including his household furnishings and his automobile—to raise the $3,400 needed to acquire his share of the startup capital.

Initially, the company was called the Continental Radio and Television Company, but in 1940, it was incorporated as the Admiral Corporation. Fortunately for the investors, the company was a success very quickly, and within two years, it had sales that exceeded $2 million. It was known for producing quality radios at affordable prices, and by 1939, it was number five in sales volume among all of the producers of radios.

The war years were good to Admiral, and it had a number of military contracts. When the war was over, Admiral branched out into the television industry, producing its first set in 1947. It soon became a leader in this burgeoning industry along with Dumont and Philco.

Many of the early Admiral television sets were table models. They had small 7-inch screens and looked a bit like the radios that Admiral had been making with the addition of a screen. Today, we might think that they look like microwave ovens, and most of them were made with Bakelite plastic cases.

The floor model set shown on page 142 is remarkable because of its Bakelite case, which is said to be the largest piece of cast Bakelite ever made. This set is model 24A12 and has a 12-inch screen. It was first made in 1949 (although some sources say 1948) and is a fine example of the television products Admiral was making at the time. Admiral also made a very similar set around 1950. It was model 20X22 and can be identified by its smaller 10-inch screen.

By 1954, Admiral had ten manufacturing plants around the world, but Japanese competition in the mid- to late '50s began to take its toll. The company struggled through the 1960s but had to sell its color picture tube business to RCA in 1971. In 1973, it was acquired by Rockwell International.

What is it worth? In working order, this Admiral model 24A12 has a value of $750 for insurance replacement purposes.

Item 40
RCA T-120 Television

Valued at $500

Black-and-white metal television on a separate wooden stand, 21 inches wide and 18 inches high. On the stand, the piece is 40 inches high. The stand has tapered legs and an X-shaped medial stretcher. There are four tuning knobs across the front, with "RCA Victor" in the center. There are two speaker openings in the top, and the set is in good condition with only a few scuffs.

What is it? RCA was founded in 1919 as a sort of radio monopoly, and David Sarnoff was named general manager. Sarnoff was born near Minsk, Russia, (now Belarus) in 1891 and immigrated to the United States in 1900. Once in this country, he had to support his family by selling Yiddish-language newspapers on the streets of New York City.

He was employed by the Marconi Wireless Company in 1906 as an office boy and became a junior telegraph operator in 1908. Sarnoff studied electrical engineering at the Pratt Institute and worked his way up the ladder at Marconi. In 1915, he proposed a device he called a "radio music box." This was very forward thinking because in 1915 radio was mainly used by shipping interests and by amateurs.

His idea was that his device would bring music into American households the way phonographs and pianos did at the time.

When Sarnoff became general manager of the newly founded RCA, he had a plan: RCA would not only manufacture radios, but they would also produce a wide range of programming such as music, sports, and news.

Within just a few years, Sarnoff's "radio music box," rechristened the "Radiola," was a big success. In 1926, as general manager of RCA, he was instrumental in forming NBC—the National Broadcasting Company—but it would not be long before Sarnoff had even bigger ideas.

Sarnoff envisioned "every farmhouse equipped not only with a sound-receiving device but with a screen that would mirror the sights of life." Vladimir Zworykin had already demonstrated his "iconoscope" camera and "kinescope" receiver, a form of early television, and Sarnoff asked Zworykin how much it would cost to produce a marketable system.

The reply was $100,000 and a year and a half—it actually took $50 million and ten years, but finally Sarnoff introduced television at the 1939 World's Fair in New York City. He announced the new technology, saying, "Now we add sight to sound." He also offered the opinion that television and television production was a "new art so important in its implications that it is bound to affect all society."

Of course, this was 1939 and World War II was already beginning, and the true burgeoning of television would have to wait until the war was over. The black-and-white set seen on page 145 was produced in 1949 and is RCA's Model T-120. The serial number on this unit is C1885924, and it was manufactured in Camden, New Jersey. This unit is in remarkable condition, but it should not be plugged in until it has been thoroughly evaluated by a specialist who will make sure that something untoward does not happen.

What is it worth? Sets of this age and condition are hard to find, and this RCA T-120 has an insurance replacement value of $500.

Item 41
RCA Color Television, "The Merrill"

Valued at $3,000
Floor-model color television by RCA,
27½ inches wide by 25 inches deep
by 39½ inches tall. It has a 15-inch
screen with a 16-position turret tuner.
It is in working order, but the feet
have been scuffed.

What is it? This set is called "The Merrill," and it is the first color television set produced by the Radio Corporation of America—better known as "RCA." It was manufactured in Bloomington, Indiana, and when it was new in 1954, it cost $1,000, which was a lot of money in post-Korean War America. It is said that 5,000 of these sets were made, but today, fewer than 120 are known to exist—and only about 25 percent are operational.

In the early 1950s, television was still somewhat in its infancy. To be sure, the German government had begun national television service in 1935, and the first regularly scheduled television broadcasts in the United States had begun just before the outbreak of World War II in 1939. In the 1940s, several commercial television stations were licensed, and monochromatic television images began to whiz through the air more and more throughout the early 1950s.

Experimentation on a color television system had begun as early as 1928, and CBS proposed its "Field Sequential System" in 1940, but it did not get on the air until 1951. In this procedure, the system broadcast the three primary colors sequentially. This required a rotating color wheel in front of the camera and another mounted in front of the television set that was synchronized to the one on the camera. Unfortunately, this color system was not compatible with the black-and-white sets then in American homes, which meant owners could not receive the color signal, much less see it on their black-and-white sets.

The Korean War delayed the development of color television somewhat, but when the smoke of battle had cleared, RCA-NBC had developed a system that allowed a signal with a color component to be received by black-and-white sets and sets that were designed to be for "color." This RCA-NBC system used the simultaneous transmission of two signals—one signal contained the brightness of the image, which could be picked up and seen as a black-and-white image, while the other signal carried the individual colors and their intensity. Put them both together, and the result was color television.

The system was called the "NTSC" color method, and it was approved by the FCC in 1953 and went into effect on January 22, 1954. Westinghouse produced the first color-compatible television, but it cost a whopping $1,295, and Admiral had an early color set that retailed for $1,175. Both of these prices were more than half of the average wage earned by American workers in a year's time.

The first units were sold in 1953 in time for some well-heeled viewers to watch the first national coast-to-coast color broadcast, which was of the 1954 Tournament of Roses Parade held on New Year's Day in Pasadena, California. By March 1954, RCA CT-100s, such as the one shown here with its 15-inch screen, were available for consumers who could afford the $1,000 price.

There was a great deal of consumer resistance to these early sets, and there were reports that homeowners were waiting for larger screens, lower prices, better color quality (the RCA NTSC system was often waggishly referred to as "Never Twice the Same Color"), and more color broadcasts. Within a year, prices on these sets were dropping precipitously and the price of CT-100 sets fell to $495. However, color television was not hugely popular and widely available until the 1960s.

What is it worth? This working RCA CT-100 with the original cabinet in excellent condition has an insurance replacement value of $3,000.

Large wooden wheel mounted on an oak base, 31 1/2 inches in diameter with a rectangular opening with rounded ends located in the lower right quadrant. The tag on top of the wheel reads "Color Converter Inc. Columbia City, Indiana." The electronics that accompany this device has seven tubes.

What is it?

This large, strange-looking device that looks as if it might make a good table top is actually an "adapter" designed to be placed in front of a black and white television to "colorize" the picture. As we have discussed earlier, color television was around in 1955 when this "Col-R-Tel" device was marketed, but it was much too expensive for the average consumer.

This wheel, which was made by Color Converter of Columbia, Indiana, was meant to be mounted over an ordinary black-and-white television set with a 10-inch screen. Behind the wheel, there was a seven-tube color converter with connections that could be attached to various parts of the television. There was also a small motor and a wheel covered with cellophane in the three primary colors—red, yellow, and blue— from which all other colors are derived. When the Col-R-Tel wheel was in motion, it spun at 600 revolutions per minute and the eye did not discern the motion or the passing colors.

The Col-R-Tel could not work unless the television set that it was attached to could receive a color signal. Monochromatic sets of the 1955 era did just that because the RCA NTSC system supplied two signals—black-and-white sets could display only the monochromatic portion, while color sets showed the entire spectrum. The Col-R-Tel worked because it could convert the color component of the signals for use on an otherwise black-and-white set.

With the Col-R-Tel, the wheel spun madly in front of the black-and-white television and a reasonable color picture was produced. According to company advertising, this is how the device worked: "The Col-R-Tel converter uses the image on an ordinary black and white tube. Feeding back to the tube video information that the set would otherwise ignore, it keys the single electron beam to the proper illumination for each color at each spot on the screen. Then it locks a three-color disk in step with the framing frequency, something like the old CBS system, producing a color picture."

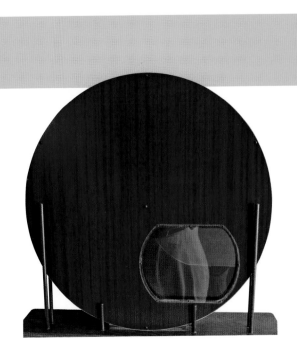

The picture produced in this manner did (according to most users) tend to be a bit dim because of the color wheel that was in front of the picture tube. To combat this problem, it was recommended that the brightness and contrast be turned up on the black-and-white set when the Col-R-Tel was in place.

When new, the Col-R-Tel sold for $150, and some assembly was required. Company literature said installation was easy if the wiring diagram for the black-and-white television being converted was at hand. The job required a soldering iron and ten connections to be made to various parts of the set. Sounds like a good way to blow up a perfectly good black-and-white television—and a color conversion apparatus.

What is it worth?
One of these recently sold on eBay for $6,800, but this example has some condition problems and should be valued somewhat less. In this condition, the insurance replacement value is $3,500.

Item 42
Philco "Predicta"

Valued at $650

Black-and-white television set with 17-inch picture tube that swivels from side to side to face the viewer. This component is mounted on a rectangular base with a built-in antenna. The metal base is perforated for cooling purposes and is dark blue with a camel-colored fabric cover over the front. There are two knobs on the front and a raised "Philco" logo. The set is in working condition.

What is it? As was discussed in the Radio section, Philco had its origins in 1892 as the Spencer Company. The name Philco first appeared in 1919 as a trade name on a battery, but the company did not become the Philco Corporation until 1940, which was sometime after the company had started experimenting with the idea of television.

While their radio business was booming, Philco began exploring the new field of television technology. For a time, it financed the work of Philo T. Farnsworth, who is credited with inventing the first electronic television apparatus in 1927.

Philco was granted a license by the FCC to open an experimental television station in 1931. By 1941, there were around 700 television sets in Philadelphia tuned to WPTZ-TV, which were the call letters for the Philco station, which operated from 1941 to 1953. During this period, viewers were served a steady diet of mainly sports programming—especially the football games of the University of Pennsylvania Quakers.

Soon, Philco was manufacturing television receivers that had small screens and were very expensive. Its first model had 61 square inches (in today's terms approximately a 7-inch screen), and it cost a whopping $349.50. Nonetheless, by the following year, Philco was turning out 800,000 sets and could not keep up with the buying public's demand for this new technology.

Philco became a leader in the television industry, but its models did not have a lot of stylistic pizzazz. When the television market slowed down in the mid-1950s, Philco felt it had to do something innovative to jumpstart sales. Part of the inspiration for the new Philco line came from the Russian satellite *Sputnik*, which was launched in 1957. After that event, there was a great deal of interest among American consumers for all things "space age." The new line was named "Predicta," and the company slogan was "TV today from the world of tomorrow."

Philco's innovative wide-deflection picture tube and printed circuits helped the designers of these modern-looking television receivers by allowing them to make sets in which the picture tube no longer had to be contained in a box-like chassis. Instead, it could be placed above or to the side of the actual receiver. This redesign opened up a number of design possibilities.

The first Predicta, which appeared in 1958, was called the "Holiday" and was designed by Richard Whipple and Severin Jonassen. The picture tube swiveled to face the viewer, and the picture tube was roughly a rectangle with rounded corners that rose above its rectangular base. This base came with a blond or mahogany finish, and the set sold for around $270.

One of the most desired of the new Philco Predicta models had the rather pedestrian name of the "Pedestal," but collectors have more imaginative designations such as the "Cyclops" or the "gas pump." This set is really more reminiscent (to us) of a lighthouse with the picture-swiveling picture tube on top and a tower-like base below. This Predicta came in a blond finish and originally cost around $460.

Other Predicta models include the "Penthouse," the "Continental," and the "Princess," which was introduced in 1959. Similar models to the "Princess" were the "Siesta," which had a clock/timer that could turn the television set on and off, and the "Debutante," which came in a variety of dramatic colors. The set shown here is an example of the Debutante.

The lifespan of the Philco's Predicta models was very short; they were discontinued in 1960. Production was stopped because the sets were expensive and had black-and-white picture tubes at a time when color television was becoming more popular and more affordable.

The Predictas also had some technical problems, and some models had picture tubes that did not perform well. This hurt Philco's reputation for quality, and to dispose of them, many Predictas were sold off in bulk to hotel chains.

Today, some collectors of television sets think that Philco Predictas are the ultimate in post–World War II television receivers, and they are very desirable on the current market. Novices should be aware, however, that new Predicta models are available which closely resemble the originals.

What is it worth? The insurance replacement value of this Philco Predicta Debutante television is $650.

Modern Age
Miscellany

Item 43

Schwinn "Aero-Cycle" Bicycle

Valued at $6,160

Schwinn boys "Aero-Cycle" bicycle with a restored aluminum color and red paint finish. It has a Delta Gangway pancake horn with push button, red B.F. Goodrich Silvertown tires, a Troxel saddle with red edging, a rear carrier and chain guard that are correct for this model bicycle, and a rear taillight. The bicycle is in excellent restored condition.

What is it?

The bicycle has its origins in the early nineteenth century, and today, it is estimated that there are more than 1 billion of these vehicles in use around the world. There are some questions about the antecedents of the bicycle—some say they go back to a 1790s device called a "dandy horse," which was invented by the French Comte de Sivrac, but today, there are doubts as to whether this ever existed.

Karl Drais, a German baron, patented a kind of bicycle in 1817. These pedal-less vehicles are called "draisines" and were propelled by the rider's feet pushing against the ground. In the 1850s and '60s, Frenchmen Ernest Michaux and Pierre Lallement pushed the concept of the bicycle forward when they designed a vehicle that had pedals on a large front wheel. These bicycles had wooden wheels with iron bands for "tires," and they were appropriately called "boneshakers."

Improvements brought to the boneshaker included solid rubber tires, a seat mounted more squarely over the pedals, and a larger front wheel. One of these bicycles was called an "ordinary." Later, these machines slowly began to approach the modern idea of what a bicycle should look like when gears were added, the size of the front wheel was reduced, and the seat was set further back. These bicycles were called "dwarf ordinaries."

Eventually, a chain and rear-wheel drive were introduced, and these bicycles became known as "dwarf safeties" or "safety bicycles." The first bicycle that many would recognize as a "modern" bicycle is said to be J.K. Starley's "Rover," which first appeared in 1885.

In the late nineteenth and early twentieth centuries, many bicycle manufacturers sprang up around the world. One of these was German maker Ignaz Schwinn, who founded his company in Chicago in 1895. Schwinn was born in Germany in 1860 and had an early interest in bicycles. He immigrated to the United States in 1891 and tried to interest American bicycle manufacturers in some of his ideas for improving bicycle design. He met with no success, and in 1895, he joined with meat packer Adolph Arnold for financial backing and formed the Arnold, Schwinn Bicycle Company.

In these early years, there was something of a bicycle boom and there were thirty factories in Chicago alone that were making bicycles. Unfortunately, this boom was fairly short lived, and by 1905, the American romance with the automobile was in full swing. Bicycle production was down by 75 percent, and eighteen of the thirty bicycle makers in Chicago were out of business. Gradually, the bicycle was becoming primarily a child's toy rather than an important mode of transportation for adults.

Undeterred, Schwinn bought out failing rivals, built a new factory, and went into the motorcycle business by forming the Excelsior-Henderson company. The Great Depression was the death knell for Schwinn's motorcycle business, and this loss of income almost killed the parent business as well.

At this time, Ignaz's son, Frank W. Schwinn, was running the firm and decided to take a bold step to confront the economic downturn of the 1930s. He traveled to Europe for inspiration and returned to the United States with ideas that would lead to a major restyling of the bicycle.

This redesigning was a bold new concept in American bicycles, and it was called the "Aero-Cycle." Schwinn had the American Rubber Company produce a 2-inch diameter balloon tire that would produce a more comfortable ride. Then, he added streamlined fenders, a false "fuel tank" on the top of the frame that harked back to the fuel tank on some motorcycles, a chrome-plated headlight, and a push-button bell.

Even in the dark days of the Depression, children loved this new look in bicycles, and those who could afford the $35 price tag had to have one. Schwinn became known as the "Cadillac" of American bicycles because of their quality and excellence in design.

What is it worth? This circa-1936 Schwinn Aero-Cycle bicycle sold at auction in 2004 for $6,160.

Item 44
Evinrude "Streamflow" Bicycle

Valued at $6,600

Boys bicycle with balloon tires, speedometer, horn, and steering lock minus its original key. The frame is made from aluminum and the red paint is a restoration.

What is it? When the name Evinrude is mentioned, outboard motors for boats immediately come to mind—not bicycles. Yet the item pictured here is a 1937 Evinrude "Streamflow" balloon tire bicycle circa 1937.

Oli Evinrude was born in a rural area north of Oslo, Norway, in 1877, but he and his family immigrated to the United States in the early 1880s and settled in Cambridge, Wisconsin. At 16, Evinrude began working in Madison, Wisconsin, in machinery stores and studied engineering on his own. In 1900, he became an engineer and pattern maker for the E.P. Allis Company in Milwaukee.

There is a story that Evinrude was rowing a boat across a lake to fetch his future wife an ice cream cone when the idea for the outboard motor came to him. In 1909, he created the first reliable, detachable outboard motor, and he and his wife marketed it to fishermen—mainly in Denmark and Norway.

Evinrude sold his company to C.J. Meyer in 1913, but in 1919, Evinrude invented a new twin-cylinder outboard engine that was more powerful and lighter in weight than his original model. Evinrude started a new company called "Elto" (for Evinrude light twin outboard) Motor Company. This company eventually absorbed the

original Evinrude Company plus the Johnson Motor Company of South Bend, Indiana.

Oli Evinrude died in 1934, and his son Ralph took over. During the years of the Great Depression, Evinrude tried everything imaginable to keep the factory open. It focused on making items such as lawnmowers, camp stoves, and bicycles that were cheaper than outboard motors and, therefore, more affordable to the strapped-for-cash American public. The bicycle was introduced in 1937 and called the "Streamflow." Today, it is very rare and valuable.

According to an Evinrude advertisement, this bicycle was "Brand new . . . brilliantly styled . . . offering revolutionary features, which contributes amazingly to riding ease and comfort." The ad concluded, "Evinrude now presents the *Streamflow Bicycle with the Full Floating level ride!,*" and went on to describe how this bicycle allowed the rider to "FLOAT over bumps and uneven pavement independent of the frame."

It was a great example of streamline design, but unfortunately, its engineering was terribly flawed and the bicycle was dangerous to ride. The bicycles broke apart while "floating over bumps," and the Evinrude Streamflow was quickly recalled by the manufacturer.

However, a few bicycle dealers kept them, and over the years, just a few have come onto the market. The example pictured here is the Imperial model of the Streamflow, which has been restored.

What is it worth?
Due to its restored condition, this Evinrude Imperial model Streamflow bicycle sold at auction in 2004 for $6,600. Another Streamflow, which is said to be the "best original unrestored Evinrude in existence," sold for $18,700—or $17,000 plus a 10 percent buyer's premium.

Item 45

Shelby "Speedline Airflow" Boys Bicycle

Valued at $6,160

Boys bicycle with streamline
styling and balloon tires. It is
fully restored in red and silver
paint.

What is it? The Shelby Cycle Company of Shelby, Ohio, produced a pneumatic tired safety bike called the "Ideal" in 1895. Over the years, the company had a number of ups and downs including a defective bicycle frame that nearly put the company out of business in 1924.

It reorganized, and in 1928, began making the "Lindy Flyer." This bicycle was named in honor of Charles Lindbergh and had a small aluminum representation of the "Spirit of St. Louis" on the front fender. It also produced the "Whippet," which had a representation of a small dog on the front fender. Shelby was successful in the 1920s, but the Great Depression put the company in great jeopardy. To stay in business, it reportedly decided to follow the lead of Schwinn's Aero-Cycles and introduced a streamlined bicycle, which it called the "Speedline Airflow." This bicycle first appeared in 1938 in a variety of colors and with a wide range of equipment.

One of the more distinctive features of the Speedline Airflow was its so-called "ram's horn" handlebars, which are clearly seen in this example. The Airflow was also distinguished by an unusually long horn tank that juts out about seven inches beyond the head tube and over the front fender.

Shelby bicycles have become very popular with collectors, who point to them as prime examples of industrial design that take on some of the aspects of art.

What is it worth? This circa-1938 restored Shelby Airflow bicycle sold at auction in 2004 for $6,160.

Related item

Girls bicycle with balloon tires. It is in fully restored condition in shades of red and silver.

What is it?
This is a circa 1938 Shelby "Speedline Airflow" girls bicycle.

What is it worth?
This bicycle sold at auction in 2004 for $1,908.

Item 46
Lighthouse
Cocktail Shaker

Valued at $900

Silver-plated cocktail shaker in the form of a lighthouse with windows up the side and around the top behind a projecting railing, 11 inches tall and missing its tower form lid. It is dated 1931 and has an inscription from the South Shores Country Club. The bottom is marked "S.P. CO. International S. Co." with a lion inside of a device that looks like a protractor.

What is it?

There is some dispute about who invented the cocktail and when. However, it is known that the first mention of the word "cocktail" occurred in the Hudson, New York, *Balance and Columbian Repository* on May 13, 1806. A puzzled reader queried the publication as to what a "cocktail" was. The paper replied that it was a "stimulating liquor, composed of spirits of any kind, sugar, water, and bitters."

It was the addition of "bitters" that made the cocktail a cocktail instead of a "punch" or a "sling." Bitters are an alcoholic concoction made from herbs and roots, and as the name suggests, they usually have a bitter flavor. One of the more famous types of bitters is Angostura Bitters, which uses gentian as the herb and was first compounded in Venezuela in 1824. In addition to cocktails, bitters were used as digestives and as patent medicine.

The origin of the word "cocktail" is open to some conjecture, but one source says it was the name given to a mixed-breed horse that had had its tail docked or cut to distinguish it from its purebred cousins. The idea is that the cocktail is a mixture just like the mixed-breed horse.

In any event, some speculate that cocktails have been around since the sixteenth century, but their great popularity had to wait for the 1920s and the introduction of Prohibition in the United States. Despite the illegality, Americans kept right on drinking booze, but the quality of the alcohol they were imbibing was generally so inferior that bartenders tried to disguise the bad taste with other ingredients that were not illegal. In other words, the cocktail became hugely popular as a means to mask the taste of "bathtub gin" and other types of substandard alcohol.

Thus, the cocktail became a part of the American culture, and we popularized these drinks in the world at large. Along with the cocktail came the cocktail shaker, although there are those who trace the development of this device back some 9,000 years to South America—but that may be something of a stretch.

The purpose of a cocktail shaker is twofold—the first is to mix the various ingredients together efficiently, and the other is to chill the liquid with the ice that is always placed in the container just before shaking. There are essentially three types of cocktail shakers: the "Boston shaker," the "cobbler shaker," and the "cocktail pitcher/shaker."

The Boston shaker is probably the earliest of the shakers and has two parts—a metal mixing vessel and a slightly smaller glass tumbler for the lid. Originally, bartenders probably used a pint beer glass to form the lid. This type of cocktail shaker does not have a built-in strainer.

The cobbler shaker is a little fancier and generally has three pieces—a metal tumbler, a lid with a built-in strainer, and a removable top that fits snuggly on the lid above the strainer. This is the type of cocktail shaker found most commonly in homes and is the type of shaker pictured here.

The third type of cocktail shaker is very similar to the cobbler type except it has a handle and a covered pouring spout jutting out from the side. These were most popular before Prohibition and may have vanished from most home bars because, with their protrusions, they can be somewhat inefficient and difficult to use.

After Prohibition ended in 1933, the public was bombarded with images of cocktails and cocktail shakers. It was almost not possible to go to a movie without seeing a bartender or the cast's "sophisticate" shaking away, making some sort of cocktail. These devices became very popular—you could not be truly urbane and chic unless you owned and knew how to use a cocktail shaker.

Cobbler-style cocktail shakers came in a wide variety of shapes and can be found in the form of golf bags, penguins, zeppelins, airplanes, and yes, lighthouses. The one shown here is known as the "Boston Lighthouse," and it was made by the International Silver Company in its Meriden, Connecticut, facility known as the Meriden Silver Plate Co.

This firm was founded in 1869 and became part of International Silver in 1898. The half circle or protractor-shaped mark found on this lighthouse cocktail shaker was not used until 1921, and the 1931 date on the piece indicates that it was made circa 1930.

This is a highly sought after form of cocktail shaker, but unfortunately, this example is incomplete. It is missing its tower-like top, and this greatly devalues this piece.

What is it worth?
This Boston Lighthouse cocktail shaker sold at auction in 2006 for $900, but a complete example has an insurance replacement value of as much as $19,000!

Related item

Two-piece cocktail mixer that consists of a silver soldered cylinder with a lid and a pouring spout, 10 inches tall and 3 inches in diameter. The lid has a round knob on three stepped rings. The body is decorated with two sets of engine-turned lines bracketing an incised stylized depiction of a train with wings. Inside of the lid are the initials "U.P.R.R." and "IS" in block letters. The base also has the initials "IS" in blocks and "International Silver Company" with "Silver Soldered" and again "U.P.R.R." The piece is in excellent condition.

What is it?

The elegant railroad dining cars of the past are now little more than a fantasy seen in old movies. In days gone by, however, the various railroad companies had rolling restaurants that were equipped with all of the items necessary to serve a fancy meal or prepare a superb cocktail.

These items generally carried the company name, often the name of the train (such as the "Twentieth Century Limited" or "Santa Fe Super Chief") and perhaps some sort of company logo. The majority of these items were made from earthenware (occasionally porcelain) and from nickel silver or silver plate.

The array of railroad silver that is available to collectors is staggering. Fairly commonly found items include coffeepots, teapots, creamers, sugar bowls, sauce boats, water pitchers, bread trays, salt and pepper shakers, syrup jugs, mustard pots, various sizes of trays, and butter pats. These were items that every train with a dining car had in abundance.

Somewhat harder to find are menu holders, flower vases, tea strainers, corn holders, and perhaps the rarest of all, cocktail shakers. Since there were only one or two of these latter items on any given train, these items can be hard to find and relatively valuable.

The Union Pacific Railroad was chartered by the U.S. Congress in 1862 as part of this nation's first transcontinental railroad line. The line was chartered to start building its railroad in Omaha, Nebraska, and lay tracks westward until it came to the California-Nevada border, where it would join with the Central Pacific Railroad, which had started its construction in Sacramento, California.

Construction on the Union Pacific began in 1865, and after much difficulty, it met the tracks of the Central Pacific just outside Ogden, Utah, on May 10, 1869. The monumental occasion of completing the first transcontinental railroad was marked by driving the famous golden spike. Union Pacific ran into financial trouble in the late nineteenth century but managed to recover. Today, it has around 33,000 miles of track located in the West, Midwest, and Gulf Coast regions.

The piece shown here was used to mix cocktails, but it was not designed to be a shaker because the pouring lip would not allow another vessel to be placed over the top to make a complete seal that would allow for vigorous shaking. If this were attempted, liquor might very well spray all over the place.

In other words, we do not believe that this is a Boston-style shaker as discussed in the previous item. Instead, it appears to be a drink mixer where concoctions were stirred to blend the ingredients and not shaken. Originally, a long bar spoon was probably used with this item.

The design shown on the side of this piece is called the "Winged Streamliner" and is most commonly associated with dining car china made by Syracuse and Scammell's Trenton China. It is a logo that is much desired by collectors, but it should be mentioned that this winged train symbol has been widely reproduced.

This silver-soldered cocktail pitcher/mixer was made by the International Silver Company, which was founded in 1898. The mark on this piece was probably not used until 1928, and this piece was made sometime during the second quarter of the twentieth century.

What is it worth?
Railroad silver cocktail mixers such as this one are considered to be quite rare, and this one is valued for insurance replacement purposes at $4,000.

Item 47

Tucker Automobile Smoking Set

Valued at $600

Heavy metal smoking set with an ashtray and cigarette box. The model of the Tucker automobile lifts up to reveal a compartment underneath to store cigarettes. It is made from pot metal that has been painted red and silver (aluminum) and has the word "Tucker" in raised letters on the edge of the ashtray.

What is it? Preston Thomas Tucker was born in Capac, Michigan, in 1903. At 16, he repaired and sold his first car, but his first real job was as a police officer. It is said that he joined the police force so that he could have access to their high-performance automobiles. But Tucker quit his job with the Lincoln Park Police Department when he was demoted for installing an unauthorized heater for more comfort during those long winter patrols in his squad car. He moved on to be a car salesman and manager of an automobile dealership located in Memphis, Tennessee.

Tucker made a pilgrimage to the Indianapolis 500 race each year, where he convinced Harry Miller, who was famous for the winning engines he built for Indy cars, to let him build a car that could and would compete in the famous race. In 1938, they formed the Miller-Tucker Company, and they secured a contract to build race cars for the Ford Motor Company. They assembled ten cars for Ford, but sadly, Tucker was once again visited with misfortune when all of the steering boxes on the cars overheated and locked up, causing the vehicles to drop out of the competition.

During World War II, American car companies were in war production and there were no new passenger car models. After the war, the public wanted something new, and in 1946, Tucker formed the Tucker Corporation to manufacture what he envisioned as an innovative motor car, which he eventually advertised as the "First completely new car in 50 years."

The "Tucker Torpedo," as it came to be known due to its streamlined design, was actually designed by Alex Tremulis, who had previously been associated with such famous car companies as Duesenberg and Cord. It took just six days to create the initial "torpedo" design, and it was hailed as a "safety car."

The initial specifications called for disc brakes, fuel-injected engine, a steering box behind the front axle that was designed to protect the driver in a crash, and a padded dashboard to help protect passengers. Another innovation was a third headlight called "The Cyclops Eye," which was designed to come on every time the car turned ten degrees or more to assist in lighting the car's way while negotiating a steep curve or turn. Some of these innovations, including the disc, did not make it into the final automobile.

The plant Tucker and his associates leased was an old Dodge aircraft plant in Chicago (Cicero), Illinois, but he and his company soon ran into all kinds of trouble with the car design and the federal government. The War Assets Administration had leased the plant to Tucker under the condition that he raise $15 million in capital by March 1, 1947. To raise the money, Tucker basically had two choices—he could relinquish control of his company to money men, or he could use some creative fundraising. Pursuant to his goal, Tucker raised $6 million by selling dealership franchises for a car that was still just on the drawing board with the money raised to be held in escrow until the cars could be delivered. Tucker also inaugurated a "Tucker Accessories Program" in which prospective buyers of the Tucker could buy accessories for the car such as a radio and seat covers. He also sold stock in one of the first speculative IPOs, or initial public offerings.

Forging ahead with the project, the Tucker Corporation prepared a prototype (dubbed the "Tin Goose") and introduced it on July 17, 1947. Three thousand people showed up—but the car nearly did not. The suspension snapped and the car would not move. Tucker talked on stage to his 3,000 guests for two hours before the car could be repaired enough to be pushed out onto a turntable.

There was a plethora of problems with the prototype, including its engine and its transmission, but eventually, fifty Tucker Torpedoes (or "Tucker '48," which was the official name) were built. This was despite Tucker's creative financing, which had caught the attention of the Securities and Exchange Commission and the company was under an investigation that would culminate in indictments for Tucker and his executives.

They would ultimately "beat the rap," but the bad publicity and the actions of the government spelled doom for Tucker, and the company went out of business. Today, forty-seven of the fifty-one Tucker automobiles are known to exist and examples have been known to have sold for as much as $700,000.

Almost any kind of Tucker memorabilia is now extremely collectible, and this smoking set composed of an ashtray and cigarette box is no exception. It is hard to know why this piece was made—it could have been intended to grace the desk of the owner of a Tucker dealership franchise, or it might have been given away as a "party favor" at the introduction of the Tucker prototype in 1947. In any event, it is a very interesting and unusual piece from the late 1940s.

What is it worth? Authentic Tucker memorabilia is hard to come by and can be rather pricey. This smoking set has an insurance replacement value of $600.

Item 48
Cleopatra's Manicure Set

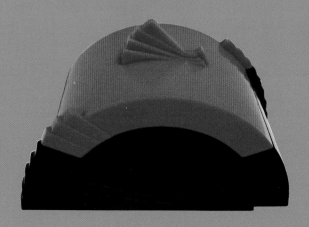

Valued at $850

Box made from black and red plastic; the box is 5¾ inches at its longest and 3½ inches at its tallest. The box is semicircular with a "swooping lines" finial that somewhat resembles a partially opened fan. The body itself is also decorated with raised "swooping lines" that resemble a partially opened fan. This piece is unmarked and in good condition.

What is it? In the 1967 movie *The Graduate*, the central character, Benjamin Braddock, is told that he should go into plastics—because that was where the future and the money were. Unfortunately, this advice was just a tad late because, by this time, plastics had been around for a very long time.

The dictionary defines "plastic" as being any of a number of complex organic compounds that are produced by polymerization, which is the process of uniting one or more "monomers," or small molecules, into a chemical "chain." Plastics are said to have a "backbone," which is a "chain" of monomers from which other monomers are hung to form the chemical structure of a plastic. More importantly perhaps, a plastic is a substance that can be molded, extruded, cast into various shapes, formed into films or sheets, and drawn into a filament or fiber.

There are naturally occurring plastics—things such as rubber, shellac, and asphalt. The first thermoplastic compound was created in 1856 by Alexander Parkes, and we know it today as "celluloid." Originally, it was called "Parkesine," and it was initially used to waterproof clothing.

In the twentieth century, the plastics revolution really began with Dr. L.H. Bakeland's 1909 invention of Bakelite, which has been discussed previously. This product was available primarily in brown and black, and used fillers such as carbon black and sawdust in the manufacturing process, which kept this material dark and opaque.

When the Bakelite patents ran their course and expired in 1927, they were acquired by the Catalin Corporation. This company modified the formula and used new coal tar dyes invented by German chemists to transform the formerly dark, opaque Bakelite into a translucent plastic that could exhibit a rainbow of colors.

This plastic, which came in an almost infinite variety of colors, was made into a vast array of objects and industrial designers explored its possibilities endlessly. This plastic was relatively easy to mass produce and was used to make fashionable costume jewelry and other objects such as the Art Deco box shown here.

Designers limited only by their imaginations and their talents used plastic to create objects in the most modern styles. American industry then mass-produced these colorful items, making them affordable to most consumers.

The box shown here is known as Cleopatra's manicure set, and it was made by General Electric's Plastics Division circa 1935. When it was new, it contained a manicure set, but now it is empty with only the fashion-forward container remaining. Today, this container makes a bold statement with its red and black color scheme and the swooping speed lines that form its decoration.

What is it worth? The insurance replacement value of this Catalin plastic box is $850.

Glossary

AIRPLANE DIAL

Often found on mid-twentieth-century radios, this term refers to a large round dial with a pointer that is calibrated for a full 360 degrees. These dials resemble those found in airplane cockpits.

AM

These two initials stand for "amplitude modulation." It is the range most radios received in the early days and is still in use today. The AM frequency range has changed as radio has evolved, but ranges from about 550 kilohertz (or kilocycles) to 1,600 kilohertz. Early on, this went up to 1,700 kilohertz and above, which allowed radios to receive the "police band" and hear emergency calls.

ART DECO

This is perhaps the most overworked and misused term in the entire world of collecting. Unfortunately, there is a great deal of disagreement as to what Art Deco actually is, when it started, or when it ended. The term per se was not in wide use until the 1960s, but it has its origins in the 1925 "Paris Exposition Internationale des Arts Decoratifs et Industriels Moderne." Shorthand for "Arts Decoratifs" became Art Deco. It should be understood, however, that Art Deco existed long before this exposition was held. There is some thought that the roots of Art Deco go back to 1909 and the bold and colorful scenery that Sergei Pavlovich Diaghilev designed for the premier appearance of the Ballet Russe in Paris. Today, we associate the term with bold colors, zigzagging and parallel lines, geometric and stylized florals, and the dancing "flapper." There are actually two branches of Art Deco design. The first features lush representations of geometrically stylized fruit and flowers and sleek human figures exemplified by women elegantly posed with wolfhounds or with women holding their skirts or long scarves as they danced or posed nude or semi-nude. The second, later branch of Art Deco grew out of a desire to create a revolution in design that took its inspiration from industry and the machine. It used straight, clean lines: squares, rectangles, chrome, glass, and no frills. Art Deco in both of its incarnations was an artists and designers movement. By the 1930s, pure Art Deco was a thing of the past, but its influence continued with such things as mid-century modernism, art moderne, and streamlining.

BAKELITE

A brand name given a type of plastic that is based on the thermosetting phenol formaldehyde resin polyoxybenzylmethylenglycolanhydride. It was developed by Dr. Leo Baekeland between 1907 and 1909. This is the first plastic made from synthetic polymers, is opaque and found in a wide variety of colors from black to red. It is very hard and durable and was used in a number of industrial applications and for making jewelry for a time.

BALLOON TIRES
On a bicycle, these are usually 2.125-inch tires with separate inner tubes and clincher rings. On classic bicycles, these were in use mainly from the 1930s to the 1950s. These are opposed to the single-tube tires that are a donut-type tire glued onto a rim with no inner tube, which were in use from the 1900s to the 1930s.

BICYCLE
A human-powered, pedal-propelled, two-wheeled vehicle. The wheels are attached to a frame with one wheel behind the other.

BREADBOARD
A type of early radio that has its components attached to a rectangular board, which often has "breadboard ends"—ends that are composed of narrow strips of wood attached to the end of the larger rectangular board with the grain running perpendicular to the grain in the main board.

CATALIN
A brand name of the Catalin Corporation for a type of plastic that is related to Bakelite. It is a phenol formaldehyde resin that is close to the composition of Bakelite but is produced by not using fillers such as sawdust or carbon black. Bakelite is typically brown or black, but Catalin in its pure state is transparent or milky white and can be dyed any number of bright colors or it can be marbleized. Catalin became available in the late 1930s and became very important for making radio cabinets starting in the 1940s.

CATHEDRAL
A type of radio that is taller than it is wide and terminates in a rounded or arched top. These look a bit like the windows found in some churches. These are sometimes called "Beehive" radios as well.

CONSOLE
In radios, this term refers to a floor model that has no feet or feet that are no more than 4 inches high. This style of cabinet became popular in the early 1930s and remained in fashion until around 1950.

CURRENT
There are primarily two types of electrical current. One is alternating current (AC), which has a magnitude and direction that vary cyclically. This type of current has a sine wave form that allows it to be transmitted down wires for long distances. The other type of current commonly referred to is direct current (DC), which is also called

"continuous current" because there is a constant flow of the electrical charge from high to low potential. In direct current, electrical charges flow in the same direction, and DC can normally be transmitted down a wire for only about one mile before it experiences excessive declines in voltage.

ELECTRICITY
A physical phenomena arising from the existence and interaction of electric charge, which is a property of certain subatomic particles (electrons and protons) that interact with electromagnetic fields to produce attractive and repulsive forces between them. The electric current that comes into our homes is a flow of this electric charge over wires.

ESCUTCHEON
To collectors, this term usually refers to a decorative or protective surround found around a keyhole. It can also refer to a shield bearing a coat of arms. But to radio enthusiasts, it is a decorative or protective surround found around a radio dial or knobs.

FM
These two initials stand for "Frequency Modulation" and in radio terminology refer to a new kind of reception and a frequency range. FM radio evolved just before the beginning of World War II, and pre-war sets (which are rare) cover the range of 42 to 50 megacycles (megahertz). As the war ended in 1945, this range was moved to 88 to 108 megacycles, which is where it remains today.

GIGAHERTZ
A measurement of electromagnetic frequency equal to 1 billion (ten to the ninth power) hertz.

HERTZ
A measurement of electromagnetic frequency equal to one wave cycle per second (the term "kilohertz" and "kilocycle" are interchangeable terms—"kilo" means 1,000).

HIGHBOY
In radios, a "highboy" is a tall unit that has four legs that are approximately half the height of the entire piece.

INCANDESCENT
A substance that emits visible light when heated. In the case of an incandescent light bulb, electricity heats a filament that is enclosed in a vacuum or a gas that will not support combustion. The heated filament then emits light.

LUCITE
Among the first plastics derived from petrochemicals, Lucite was discovered in 1931 by DuPont chemists working on high-pressure technology developed for ammonia production. It is a methyl

methacrylate polymer that is crystal clear and very strong. It was used extensively during World War II for windshields, nose cones, and gunner's turrets. Later, it became popular for use in more decorative applications such as lamps, tables, and even jewelry.

PLATEN
The roller on a typewriter around which the paper is wound and upon which the keys strike.

RADIO
A term derived from the word "radioconductor," which was coined by French physicist Edouard Branly in 1897 and was taken from the verb "to radiate." The word "radio" used as a noun is said to have first appeared in 1907 in an article by Lee de Forest and was adopted by the U.S. Navy in 1912.

REVOLVING LOOPER
A device on a sewing machine invented by James E.A. Gibbs that pulled up a precise quantity of needle thread in proportion to the length of the stitch to be made.

SHORT-WAVE
This refers to radio reception that is just above the AM band and goes from around 1,600 kilocycles (or kilohertz) to 30 megacycles. In the past, this was sometimes called "foreign broadcast."

SLIDE-RULE DIAL
This is a type of radio dial that is long, narrow, and rectangular and is typically placed horizontally on the radio. It resembles a slide rule and has a sliding indicator that is also reminiscent of the type found on slide rules. The original "slide rule" was an analog computer widely used by engineers and other scientists until the units became obsolete in the 1970s.

TOMBSTONE
A type of radio with a tall rectangular shape that is taller than it is wide and essentially flat on the top (some may have slightly curved or shaped tops). These get their name because they are said to resemble a tombstone, but they are also called "upright table models."

TYPEWRITER
A mechanical, electromechanical, or electronic device with a set of keys that can be depressed in some manner to print characters on paper or some other medium. When this machine first came on the market, the person who operated it was also referred to as a "typewriter."

Photo Credits

Item 1 Grover and Baker Sewing Machine
Item courtesy of the collection of Mr. Kipper Evans
Photo by Richard H. Crane

Item 2 "Florence" Sewing Machine
Item and photo courtesy of Breker Auction Team Koln (Auktionen
Uwe Breker), Cologne, Germany

Item 3 American Sewing Machine
Item and photo courtesy of Breker Auction Team Koln (Auktionen
Uwe Breker), Cologne, Germany

Item 4 Wheeler and Wilson Sewing Machine
Item and photo courtesy of Breker Auction Team Koln (Auktionen
Uwe Breker), Cologne, Germany

Item 5 Wilcox and Gibbs Sewing Machine
Item and photo courtesy of Breker Auction Team Koln (Auktionen
Uwe Breker), Cologne, Germany

Item 6 Singer Featherweight Sewing Machine
Item and photo courtesy of Mrs. D.E. Rosson Sr.
Photo by Richard H. Crane

Item 7 Singer Miniature Sewing Machine
Item and photo courtesy the collection of Elaine Tomber-Tindell

Item 8 Odell Typewriter
Item and photo courtesy of Breker Auction Team Koln (Auktionen
Uwe Breker), Cologne, Germany

Item 9 "Edison-Mimeograph" Typewriter
Item and photo courtesy of Breker Auction Team Koln (Auktionen
Uwe Breker), Cologne, Germany

Item 10 "The Baltimore" Typewriter
Item and photo courtesy of "Treasures in Your Attic"™

Item 11 Underwood #5 Typewriter
Item and photo courtesy of "Treasures in Your Attic"™

Related item #11R "Smith Premier No. 1" Typewriter
Item and photo courtesy of Breker Auction Team Koln (Auktionen
Uwe Breker), Cologne, Germany

Item 12 Edison Standard Phonograph Model "A"
Item and photo courtesy of Breker Auction Team Koln (Auktionen
Uwe Breker), Cologne, Germany

Item 13 Columbia Graphophone
Item and photo courtesy of Breker Auction Team Koln (Auktionen
Uwe Breker), Cologne, Germany

Related item #13R Reginaphone
Item and photo courtesy of Skinner Inc., Boston and Bolton,
Massachusetts

Item 14 RCA Portable Phonograph
Item and photo courtesy of Skinner Inc., Boston and Bolton,
Massachusetts

Item 15 Edison Manufacturing Company Fan
Item and photo courtesy of Skinner Inc., Boston and Bolton,
Massachusetts

Item 16 Westinghouse Fan
Item courtesy of Rex and Peggy Rule, Shepard Inn, Dandridge,
Tennessee
Photograph by Richard H. Crane

Item 17 Diehl Electric Fan
Item courtesy of Rex and Peggy Rule, Shepard Inn, Dandridge,
Tennessee
Photograph by Richard H. Crane

Item 18 "Blue Willow" Toaster
Item and photo courtesy of Breker Auction Team Koln (Auktionen
Uwe Breker), Cologne, Germany

Related item #18R Porcelier Toaster
Item and photo courtesy of Breker Auction Team Koln (Auktionen
Uwe Breker), Cologne, Germany

Item 19 Westinghouse "Turnover Toaster"
Item and photo courtesy of "Treasures in Your Attic"™

Item 20 Elekthermax Toaster
Item and photo courtesy of the Kirkland Museum of Fine and
Decorative Arts, Denver, Colorado, the Burton and Helaine
Fendelman Collection

Item 21 General Electric Toaster
Item courtesy of the collection of Roger Welsh
Photograph by Richard H. Crane

Item 22 "Twin-O-Matic" Waffle Maker
Item and photo courtesy of the Kirkland Museum of Fine and
Decorative Arts, Denver, Colorado, the Burton and Helaine
Fendelman Collection

Item 23 Coffee Urn
Item courtesy of Maria Mandojano
Photograph by Richard H. Crane

Item 24 "Kitchen Aid" Coffee Mill
Item courtesy the collection of Elaine Tomber-Tindell
Photograph by Richard H. Crane

Item 25 Dormeyer Mixer
Item and photo courtesy of the Kirkland Museum of Fine and
Decorative Arts, Denver, Colorado, the Burton and Helaine
Fendelman Collection

Item 26 Sunbeam "Mixmaster"
Item and photo courtesy the collection of Elaine Tomber-Tindell
Photograph by Richard H. Crane

Item 27 "Juice-O-Mat"
Item and photo courtesy of the Kirkland Museum of Fine and
Decorative Arts, Denver, Colorado, the Burton and Helaine
Fendelman Collection

Related item #27R "Sunkist Juiceit"
Item courtesy the collection of Elaine Tomber-Tindell
Photograph by Richard H. Crane

Item 28 "Petipoint" Iron
Item and photo courtesy of the Kirkland Museum of Fine and
Decorative Arts, Denver, Colorado, the Burton and Helaine
Fendelman Collection

Related item #28R "American Beauty" Iron
Item courtesy the collection of Elaine Tomber-Tindell
Photograph by Richard H. Crane

Item 29 "Breadboard" Radio
Item courtesy of the collection of Julian Burke
Photograph by Richard H. Crane

Related item #29R Atwater Kent "Battery Set" Radio
Item courtesy of the collection of Julian Burke
Photograph by Richard H. Crane

Item 30 Philco "Cathedral" Radio
Item courtesy of the collection of Julian Burke
Photograph by Richard H. Crane

Item 31 Zenith "Waltons" Radio
Item courtesy of the collection of Julian Burke
Photograph by Richard H. Crane

Related item #31R Philco "Tombstone" Radio
Item courtesy of the collection of Julian Burke
Photograph by Richard H. Crane

Item 32 Zenith Console Radio
Item courtesy of the collection of Julian Burke
Photograph by Richard H. Crane

Item 33 Sparton "Bluebird" Radio
Item and photo courtesy of Ivey-Selkirk Auctioneers, St. Louis, Missouri

Item 34 Majestic "Charlie McCarthy" Radio
Item courtesy of the collection of Julian Burke
Photograph by Richard H. Crane

Item 35 Emerson "Snow White" Radio
Item courtesy of the collection of Julian Burke
Photograph by Richard H. Crane

Item 36 Fada "Bullet" Radio
Item courtesy of the collection of Julian Burke
Photograph by Richard H. Crane

Related item #36R Fada "Bell" Radio
Item courtesy of the collection of Julian Burke
Photograph by Richard H. Crane

Item 37 Garod "Commander" Radio
Item courtesy of the collection of Julian Burke
Photograph by Richard H. Crane

Item 38 Coca-Cola Cooler Radio
Item courtesy of the collection of Julian Burke
Photograph by Richard H. Crane

Item 39 Admiral Bakelite Television
Item and photo courtesy of "Treasures in Your Attic"™

Item 40 RCA T-120 Television
Item and photo courtesy of the collection of Jennifer Mass

Item 41 RCA Color Television, "The Merrill"
Item courtesy of the collection of Julian Burke
Photograph by Richard H. Crane

Related item #41R "Col-R-Tel" Color Converter
Item courtesy of the collection of Julian Burke
Photograph by Richard H. Crane

Item 42 Philco "Predicta"
Item and photo courtesy of Jim Elkind, Lost City Arts, New York, New York

Item 43 Schwinn "Aero-Cycle" Bicycle
Item and photo courtesy of Copake Auction Inc., Copake, New York

Item 44 Evinrude "Streamflow" Bicycle
Item and photo courtesy of Copake Auction Inc., Copake, New York

Item 45 Shelby "Speedline Airflow" Boys Bicycle
Item and photo courtesy of Copake Auction Inc., Copake, New York

Related item #45R Shelby "Speedline Airflow" Girls Bicycle
Item and photo courtesy of Copake Auction Inc., Copake, New York

Item 46 Lighthouse Cocktail Shaker
Item and photo courtesy of Ivey-Selkirk Auctioneers, St. Louis, Missouri

Related item #46R Union Pacific Railroad Cocktail Shaker
Item and photo courtesy of Sandi Berman, Deco Deluxe, New York, New York

Item 47 Tucker Automobile Smoking Set
Item and photo courtesy of "Treasures in Your Attic"™

Item 48 Cleopatra's Manicure Set
Item courtesy of Burton and Helaine Fendelman
Photograph by Richard H. Crane

Index

Bibliography and Additional Reading

Bays, Carter. *The Encyclopedia of Early American Sewing Machines.* Columbia, S.C., Collector Books, 1993.

Bunis, Marty & Sue. *Collector's Guide to Transistor Radios, Identification and Value Guild.* Paducah, Ky., Collector Books, 1996.

Duncan, Alastair. *Modernism Modernist Design 1880–1940*, Antique Collectors' Club, Suffolk, England, 1998.

Fabrizio, Timothy C. and George F. Paul. *The Talking Machine: An Illustrated Compendium 1877–1929. Second Edition.* Atglen, Pa., Schiffer Publishing Ltd., 2005.

Greguire, Helen. *Collector's Guide to Toasters and Accessories, Identification and Values.* Paducah, Ky., Collector Books, 1997.

Hanks, David A. and Hoy, Anne. *American Streamlined Design: The World of Tomorrow*, Flammarion, Paris, France, 2005.

Johnson, David and Betty. *Guide to Old Radios, Pointers, Pictures and Prices.* Radnor, Pa., Wallace-Homestead Book Company, 1989.

L-W Books. *Evolution of the Bicycle.* Gas City, Ind., L-W Books, 1991.

L-W Books. *Evolution of the Bicycle, Volume 2.* Gas City, Ind., L-W Books, 1993.

L-W Books. *Toasters and Small Kitchen Appliances, A Price Guide.* Gas City, Ind., L-W Books, 1995.

Russo, Thomas A. *Mechanical Typewriters, Their History, Value, and Legacy.* Atglen, Pa., Schiffer Publishing Ltd., 2002.

Slusser, John and Staff of "Radio Daze." *Collector's Guide to Antique Radios, Identification and Values, 6th Edition.* Paducah, Ky., Collector Books, 2005.

Thomas, Glenda. *Toy and Miniature Sewing Machines, Identification & Value Guide, Book II.* Paducah, Ky., Collector Books, 1997.

Witt, John M. *Collector's Guide to Electric Fans Identification and Values.* Paducah, Ky., Collector Books, 1997.